Stay L and Circle Left

The Story

of

Floyd "Bad News" Winter

By

Floyd Winter and Daniel DiMarzio

Foreword by Randy Couture

Stay Low and Circle Left
The Story of Floyd "Bad News" Winter

By Floyd Winter and Daniel DiMarzio

Published by the *Winds of Japan Shop*

Copyright © 2021 by Floyd Winter and Daniel DiMarzio
ISBN 9798593627797

All Rights Reserved. No part of this book may be reproduced in any form without the express written permission of the authors.

Authors: Floyd Winter and Daniel DiMarzio

Dedicated to my children and my wife, Paula Winter. Without her I would never have accomplished what I did. She is my better half, the love of my life, and my biggest supporter.

~ Floyd Winter

Contributors

Thank you to all those who contributed to this book. My apologies if I missed any names.

Chuck Africano
Joel Bane
Gary Barber
Phil Brown
Randy Couture
Ted Cuneo
Jim Diehl
Venecom Griffin
Dr. Walter Grote
Marc Grunseth
Tom Hlavacek
Webbie Loyd
Bill Martel
Chris Pease
Pat Plourd
David Schutter
Daryl Schwartz
Ed Steers
Van Stokes
Tony Thomas
Derrick Waldroup
Jennifer Winter

Contents

Foreword   7

The Coach

Chapter 1   13

Age of Innocence

Chapter 2   18

Life and Death in Vietnam

Chapter 3   36

Back from the Jungle

Chapter 4   43

Gold in Turkey

Chapter 5   55

Love at First Sight

Chapter 6   68

Stay Low and Circle Left

Chapter 7   75

The Full-Time Coach

Chapter 8   97

Concord Cup

Chapter 9   ***109***

Globe Trotting

Chapter 10   ***117***

Golden Years

Afterword   ***128***

Lives Touched by Floyd "Bad News" Winter

Foreword

The Coach

Floyd "Bad News" Winter

My name is Randy Couture. Some may know me from my successes in Mixed Martial Arts. Some may remember me from my time on the U.S. National wrestling team or on the mat at Oklahoma State. I hope you enjoy this book about one of the biggest influences on my journey toward success.

I believe there are a few people in our journey through this world who affect us deeply. They change your perspective and even your trajectory in life. Most of us do not recognize how important those people were in our development till much later when the dust of those challenges, trials, and tribulations settles and we can look back.

Coach Floyd Winter was that for me and many of the young men who served and wrestled for the U.S. Army, the Armed services, and the U.S. National team. I have met countless others who served before me and after me whom Coach Winter, or as he is affectionately known in wrestling circles, "Bad News", affected in a similar fashion.

I was stationed at Fliegerhörst Kasern, near Haunau, West Germany. I was a new Private in a foreign country and I am not sure I could find my ass with both hands without help. I was a one-time state champion from Lynnwood, Washington.

I received no attention from college wrestling coaches and had a brand-new family to support. The Army, not wrestling, was going to make that possible. Although as a child I had dreams of being an Olympic skier just like the Mahre brothers, Olympic wrestling had never crossed my mind.

Then I met Coach Winter in the fall of 1984 at a wrestling clinic in Baumholder. Coach was teaching the tactics, technique, and rules for the two Olympic styles of wrestling, Freestyle and Greco-Roman. He had a keen wit and special flair, especially for Greco-Roman wrestling. He informed all in attendance that the Armed Forces Championship for Greco-Roman was in fact an Olympic qualifier for the trial process to make the U.S. Olympic team.

I had no experience in Greco or Freestyle but I loved the sport of wrestling and was motivated by a new vision of being an Olympic athlete. I began wrestling in every tournament I could get to and learning as much as possible about these new wrestling styles. I even joined the local German club team, TG Langendiebach, to get more mat time.

It would be another year before I saw Coach Winter again and this time it would be at the finals of the U.S. Army European wrestling championship. I won the Freestyle championship and took 2nd in the Greco. Coach Winter let me know I had done well enough to try out for the All Army team.

If I made it through the trial process and made the team, I would get the chance to compete in the Inter Service Championship wrestling against the other three service teams: Navy, Air Force, and Marines. I was off and running toward my new Olympic dream on a wrestling mat and Coach Winter was going to be the catalyst for my success.

Now, I could go on about my successes and failures on this journey. That would carry us through the 2000 Olympic trials for the United States team, but that is another book entirely. Coach Winter saw in me the passion and desire to compete with everything I was. He not only instilled in me the tactics and techniques to succeed but developed the work ethic and mindset to go with those attributes.

I never made the Olympic team. Through Coach Winter, I developed the confidence and belief in myself to compete on an international stage in an individual combative sport. I learned that a champion's character is not tested when he wins. A champion's character is tested by how he faces the adversity of loss.

Those valuable lessons from a great coach and an even better man allowed me to win with grace and humility and lose with dignity and a diligent mindset in the toughest sport on the planet. Thanks, Coach, for always being there whether I was at the top or struggling to get there.

~ Randy Couture
Las Vegas, Nevada
November 2020

Ode to the Coaches
By
Randy Couture

"A tribute to my Army wrestling coach, Floyd Winter, and all the wrestling coaches I had through my career who taught me so much! Thank you!

This is an ode to all those who have never asked for one. A thank you in words, to all those who do not do, what they do so well, for the thanking.

This is to the coaches; This is to the ones who watch our hands raised, or our face fall, at the end of each match; Who harmonize in our shared pain and sheer joy and terrified wonder as we walk to the center of the mat.

This is to the coaches; To the ones who shout the loudest and fight the hardest and sacrifice the most to prepare us for combat and ultimately success throughout all our lives.

This is to the coaches; This is to the ones with so much pride for us that they cannot fit it inside their chests after all they have endured, to the leaking of blood and wiping of sweat from the back of their hands, to so many trails from so many mops pushed across mats left behind and the tape laid on the cracks to ensure we remain injury-free as they smile through those training sessions and always manage a laugh.

This is to the coaches; This is to the patience and perseverance and unyielding dedication that they have given willingly to see us succeed in grappling competition, for all the whistles blown, drop steps and back steps and headlocks and arm drags and slide bys and duck unders and single legs and double legs shown slowly by the numbers just so we could grasp and understand and then call them our own.

This is to the coaches; For all the uniforms handed out and per diem divvied, for all the trips, trains, planes, buses, cars, and hotels booked. This is for the counseling sessions, motivational speeches, slaps on the back and moments of encouragement for one more sprint or one more minute in the grind or round robin.

This is to the coaches; This is for all those arguments; some with all those referees over every single passivity or point given or taken away. Some with wives, over family time missed, or vacations not taken for the sake of the team.

This is to the coaches; To those who demonstrate a character of the highest order and passed on a fire and a passion for the greatest sport in man's history!
To the ones who show us the way to find our own way. This is to the coaches."

Coach Floyd Winter's Award Presentation

29th Military World Wrestling Championships

October 5th, 2014

Chapter 1
Age of Innocence

I was born on May 1st, 1947, in Porterville, California, to Floyd and Aline Winter. Porterville is a small town in the San Joaquin Valley, surrounded by orange trees, grape vineyards, and olive trees. It was an idyllic setting, a rural and quiet place to grow up, sitting about halfway between Los Angeles and San Francisco.

There was only one hospital in the tiny town where I was born. I met my best friend, John Webb Loyd (aka "Webbie"), in Porterville as a young child. We always told people we were born in the same bed because we had only one hospital. That would get us a lot of strange looks. I would continue to be best friends with Webbie for the next 65 years, never once having an argument or fight. I tended to develop strong bonds with people I cared for in childhood and this would continue the rest of my life.

Living in Porterville, life was simple. It was a small town where everybody knew each other. It was just an innocent, fun time for us growing up there as young boys. I had two brothers, one sister and was the oldest in the family.

I spent time hanging out at friends' houses or having them over. I was with Webbie virtually every day throughout elementary, middle, and high school. In the 8th grade Webbie got a pool table in his basement. We would play pool every weekend until 3:00 or 4:00 AM, one time playing 24 hours straight. We went to the movies in 1962 and saw "The Hustler" and that motivated us. Webbie and I became pretty good pool players. When I became tired of playing with the pool cue I would throw it away and grab a wet mop handle, picture frame, or whatever I could find to try to best the other unsuspecting player.

While in high school I took a liking to sports. On the weekends Webbie and I would play pick-up football and basketball games with college kids we nicknamed "The Bull" and "The Rhino." We held our own against the older guys.

Having said that, I was not a great athlete, I did not have the speed. My friends did, though, and they made the track and field team. I still wanted to join the team because my friends were on it. The only way I made the track team was they had an event called "The Walk." It was heel-to-toe walking. Nobody did that, everybody ran, high-jumped, long-jumped or pole vaulted. But I did not have the skills for that. So, I did "The Walk." I actually won several of the meets because I was the only one in the event.

I wrestled in high school but I did not have a lot of talent. I probably won more than half the matches but did not win the league. I was not bad but that was the extent of my wrestling. I did not get the chance to wrestle in junior high, not because I did not want to, but the opportunity was not available back then. Now you can wrestle when you are three hours old, come out of the womb bridging.

I also played football. Junior year I made All Valley. I had an inspirational coach named Sim Ennis. He was a big guy, standing 6'6" and weighing in at 290 pounds. While in college, Sim Ennis won an Olympic gold medal in the discus in 1952 in Melbourne, Australia. I learned a great deal from this amazing coach. I did rather well in football. I actually knew the plays and could hear them being called. So, I was there before the ball was and could make the tackle.

Porterville continued to be an ideal place for me to grow up. There was a big lake eight miles from my home toward the mountains, Success Lake, where I would spend time swimming with my friends on the weekends. However, Webbie and I did manage to get into some mischief from time to time.

We had a friend named Gary Dove. He had a girlfriend who lived about 20 miles away in the foothills of the mountains. He told us where he was going to park and make out one night. So Webbie and I decided to get some stockings to put over our faces, and a starter pistol. We both jumped out of the dark, terrifying the couple making out, with me holding the starter pistol. I shot the pistol and Webbie fell over like he had been hit. As you can imagine, the girl was terrified and screaming hysterically. We thought it was funny, but her parents did not. Looking back, we probably should not have done that.

Besides the occasional teenage stunt, life was calm and tranquil in the small town. I did not know much about life, but those were some of the best times of my life. The innocence was important. Living in Porterville, it was just a really innocent time. We did not know what drugs were in high school. I did not know what marijuana was. We did not drink or smoke.

My junior year of high school things started to go downhill at home. My parents began to bicker and fight. Eventually, this led to them getting a divorce. Both of my parents were from Oklahoma and my father served in World War II. There was no opportunity for them in Oklahoma, so they had moved to California for work. Unfortunately, the marriage did not last.

This was a difficult time for me and the divorce really impacted my life. One day, at the end of my junior year in high school, I saw a commercial on TV. It was an Army advertisement about being a paratrooper and jumping out of planes. This intrigued me at my young age. I thought that was exciting stuff. Things were not going well at home and I decided I wanted to leave my small town and see the world. The Army was my ticket out.

I made the decision, and being only 17 years old at the time, my mother had to sign for me. I joined the Army. The

Vietnam war was raging and I would soon become a part of it.

Porterville was the only home I had ever known. It had been good to me up until my parents' divorce. I was only 17 and would not graduate from high school. I would trade in the orange trees, grape vineyards, and olive trees of Porterville for the dangerous jungles of Vietnam. The stark contrast between these two places could not have been more different. I was stepping into the unknown, and was eager to begin my new life with the United States Army.

Chapter 2
Life and Death in Vietnam

Eighteen-year-old Floyd Winter after surviving an ambush in Vietnam

I was still just a young boy in high school when it came time for me to ship out for the Army. It was quite a shock for me. I really had no idea what I was getting myself into and would never look at life the same again.

The Army was something I was interested in and always wanted to do. I was yelled and screamed at during most of my time at basic training in Fort Ord. My most vivid memories are of doing non-stop pushups. At Fort Benning I was the youngest soldier there. I spent three weeks doing physical training and learning how to jump out of planes. From there I moved on to Fort Campbell, Kentucky, turning 18 years old in May of 1965.

I can remember my best friend Webbie sending me the 1965 school yearbook. At the same time, we had this meeting with the Platoon Sergeant. He was a regular, mean-ass Platoon Sergeant. He actually jumped in Korea on a couple of combat jumps. I was so excited about getting the yearbook that I was looking at it while he was talking. He got pissed off and I had to do KP (Kitchen Police) or something for a few days for not listening to him. I spent a year there with the Screaming Eagles and then I got orders to go to Vietnam. I left on December 31st.

On my way to Saigon, my connection got delayed in the Seattle airport for four or five hours. Not being one to sit around, I convinced my friend to catch a taxi with me to a nearby bar. Even though I looked like I was only thirteen, they served me, and I sat down with my friend to drink some beer.

A couple girls entered the bar and my buddy and I started talking to them. We spent an hour talking, and when it was time for us to leave, one of the girls gave me her address. She wanted me to write to her from Vietnam.

Later on, when I got to Vietnam, I wrote to her. She wrote me back. We kept this going for a whole year. When I returned a year later, we got married. However, that is a story for another time.

January 1st, I landed in Tan Son Nhut Air Base in Saigon. You had to spend three or four days there because that is where you processed. They sat you down to make your last will. They asked what your blood type was, who your parents were, things like that. They also gave you some medical shots.

It was extremely hot there. There was a lot of dust flying around from the helicopters and vehicles moving all over the place. On the third day I was sent to Phan Rang, the headquarters of the 101st Brigade. I flew there in a Caribou aircraft. I got my first real look at Vietnam from the air.

Vietnam

Phan Rang was a base camp not too far from the ocean. That is where the Brigade was stationed. From there we would go on different missions all over Vietnam.

I got there and had to pull guard duty. Right away they put me where the wire was and it was a very frightening experience. I made it through fine, though. Anyway, one good thing was the beer was only a nickel there.

By this time, I still had not gotten all of my equipment yet. I was missing ammo pouches and the suspenders you hang your grenades on, stuff like that. They took me to this place where there was a big pile of stuff.

All types of military equipment were on this mound. It smelled and there were flies buzzing all over the place. It was equipment from soldiers who had been killed or severely wounded. It was their stuff. I went over and picked out the equipment that I needed. It was quite a surreal experience.

I spent a week in Phan Rang and we went out on different missions. We went to Tuy Hoa, which is a big city right on the coast. We could not drive there. It was too risky because of ambushes. We caught a Navy ship, an LST, one of those ships that carries vehicles, tanks, and other equipment. We drove our vehicles down and they lowered the front door and we drove our vehicles into the belly of the ship. It was only supposed to take eight hours to get down to the city. There was a big storm and for security reasons we had to stay out in the China Sea. That was the first time I had ever been on a boat like that.

The galley where you ate was four floors down. You got all the smells from them cooking the food. You also had other smells; of soldiers vomiting. I needed some air because I was going to puke myself, so I ran for the railing. I learned something I will never forget that day…*do not throw up into the wind.*

We landed at Tuy Hoa and spent two days securing a nearby area, setting up the perimeter. There was another place 20 miles up toward the mountains called Tuy An, which was where they grew rice. The Viet Cong were coming there and taking the rice from the villagers. So, we had our battalion go up there to secure the area.

We drove our trucks up there and set up a perimeter. During the night we would go out on long-range patrols and set up ambushes. We did not travel much during the day. We did that for several days.

You do not get to shower while you are out there. You are going through water, mud, and being eaten alive by insects. You have the same socks on for several days.

I came back from one of these long-range patrols and they were looking for volunteers to drive the trucks back down to Tuy Hoa to get supplies. That is a big city so they have showers there, the food is good, and the beer is cold. So, I volunteered to go.

My job was to sit on a jeep that was in the lead. The Viet Cong would put mines in the road. You could tell when they put mines because there was fresh dirt. We would stop and I would take the mine detector and find the mines and blow them in place.

It was an extremely hot day again and I was setting up near the jeep with the mine detector. I had not showered in a week and I was looking forward to getting to Tuy Hoa. The next thing I knew, I was thrown in front of the jeep, and the vehicle ran over me!

I was on the side of the road, dazed, not knowing what was going on. I heard some explosions and gunfire. I tried to get my rifle, but it was broken in half, having been run over by the jeep. I crawled into a ditch, keeping a low profile.

The ambush by the Viet Cong only lasted about two minutes. They could not withstand anything longer than that as we would call in artillery and airstrikes. It was a hit-and-run attack.

When the jeep hit me and I was thrown forward, I landed on my face and skinned my face up. It was like a bad burn on my face. My ribs hurt. I knew I was okay, but the driver was killed. The Lieutenant sitting next to him was severely wounded.

They called in a medivac, a dustoff. They came in and picked us up. They loaded me into the helicopter. Besides being ambushed and injured, I had not slept in a few days. The chopper blades quickly lulled me to sleep.

I was in between the severely wounded Lieutenant and the driver, who was dead. Their blood oozed all over me, mixing with mine as I slept. I had not changed clothes in a long time and my face was severely skinned. When the helicopter landed, someone grabbed my leg and I let out an "Ow!" and the next thing I heard was, "We have a live one here!"

When they brought me out of the helicopter, they had a priest read me my last rites and a doctor there. They started the process right there when I got off the chopper. They put me on a gurney and the priest and doctor were both looking at me. I looked like I was near death because I had been injured, fallen asleep, and was covered in the other soldiers' blood, as well as mine.

They took me to the hospital and cut off my uniform and boots. They asked me if I was shot and what had happened. I told them that I was okay, I knew I was not seriously hurt. They still took me into the emergency room. The doctor there asked me, "Where'd you get these skid marks on your ass?" I told him I was run over by a jeep and he laughed.

I told them I was okay and after being checked out they sent me to this ward. I was able to take a shower and they gave me clothes. On the second day, there was this Lieutenant, who was the paymaster, visiting patients. He was paying all the wounded soldiers. He gave me a hundred dollars.

Over there, a hundred dollars is a lot, especially on the black market. I was able to leave the ward, buy some clothes, and get a hop back to my unit. This hop was going to stop at another city on the coast on the way.

I got off at the city on the coast and found a hotel. I spent the next three days sitting on the beach drinking beer. Most people did not know if I was alive or dead at this point.

When I was in Vietnam, I was the only white guy in my squad. Out of ten people the rest were all African Americans. Growing up in Porterville, California, we had a student body of 2,000 at our high school. We only had two African Americans in the whole school and they were brothers.

We did not even know what it was to be prejudiced. It was a rural, agricultural area and we were just innocent kids. I did not know what soul music was until I got into the Army. The guys in my unit would be listening to James Brown and Wilson Pickett. They told me they had turned me into a "Soul brother."

Once reunited with my platoon, we were out again humping it for days in the jungles of Vietnam. You cross many rivers when you are venturing through the countryside. We had stopped to take a defensive position. A man who was in the lead came back and said, "Is anybody a good swimmer here?" In the Army there is a saying that you should *"Never volunteer for anything."* I did not heed this advice. I spoke up and said, "Yeah, I'm a pretty good swimmer."

Soldiers carrying a wounded comrade through the swamps of Vietnam

What happened was, the night before, they had a patrol that went into a river. Each soldier was carrying about 80 pounds of equipment with their weapons, ammo, food, mortars, and so on. One of the soldiers had slipped, and unfortunately, drowned.

They needed someone to go into the river and see if they could retrieve his body. They tied a rope to me and I went into the river. I could not see anything in the water because it was so murky. I could not even see my hand in front of my face. I was just pretty much feeling my way around, trying to find the soldier's body. When I found him, I was going to tie a rope to him so he could be pulled up out of the water.

I did not see or feel anything the first time, so I came back up. I went down a second time. I was feeling around, when all of a sudden, I felt something move! It scared the hell out of me.

It turned out I was swimming in the river with a giant python! I turned around and made it out of that river in about two seconds, I could have had the World Record for speed swimming.

What had happened was they had thrown grappling hooks in to try to snare the soldier's body before I dove in. Instead, they had ensnared a huge python and I found it when I went in. They eventually dragged the python out and it was enormous, over 20 feet long.

That was my first wrestling match in Vietnam. We killed the monstrous snake. Then we chopped it up, cooked it in some sauce, and ate it with rice. It was not that bad.

As an American soldier in Vietnam, I was there for about a year. We had the best medical care and food the American government could afford us. The C-rations were not the best but when you are out in the jungles and the fields, they were decent. We really had it easy compared to the South Vietnamese Army.

A soldier keeping track of the time he has left to serve in Vietnam on his helmet

The South Vietnamese soldiers had to serve six years. Their food was whatever they could find in the jungle. If they wanted to see their family, they had to travel with them.

Their families would follow in the rear. They were our partners over there fighting with us against the North Vietnamese and Viet Cong. The South Vietnamese really had it hard.

Young Vietnamese widow with a photo of her missing husband

They were really tough soldiers. I remember one time we had this South Vietnamese soldier with us. He was carrying his rucksack, ammo, water, and a base to a 4.2 mortar that weighed about 80 pounds through the jungle. He only weighed around 120 pounds.

I was amazed by his strength to be able to carry all that. He never asked for any help. I offered to help him but he refused. The things that they would have to eat were horrible. He found this furry insect and put it in his mouth and started chewing it. He found another one and offered it to me but I said, "No, thank you!"

They did not have good medical care either. They did not have helivacs or anything to chopper you off to the hospital to see a doctor. Everything they had was in the field with them with their own medics. Life was very hard for them.

When you were halfway through your tour you usually got to take R & R. In July of 1966 I went on R & R. I caught a flight and went to Penang, which is an island off Thailand. The only thing I had was a small duffel bag and jungle fatigues.

They got us a nice hotel with hot food and showers. I was able to go out and buy some civilian clothes. I was there for four or five nights. They actually had a lot of Australians on the island because they were fighting in Borneo. I made friends with an Australian Captain while I was there.

He invited me to go to their Officer's Club one night. He picked me up and drove me to the Australian Airbase. We went to their Officer's Club, and compared to being out in the jungle it was great. It was a lot of fun meeting different Australians.

The Captain had a girlfriend who had a younger sister. She was about my age. I met her and we kind of hit it off. I got her phone number and called her the next day. I asked her if she wanted to go out for dinner. She told me she had to ask her father. Her father said that he would rather have me come over to his house.

He had a car pick me up the next day. They lived in this beautiful mansion overlooking the ocean. I noticed when I went in that they had butlers and maids. We had cocktails and ate dinner.

One thing that was unique about this girl was that her name was Constantina. That sounded to me just like "Concertina", the name of the barbed wire you put out in front of your position that is razor sharp, so your position does not get overrun.

After dinner, Constantina played the piano for us. The next day I took her out for dinner and bought her a dress that she liked. We even took one of those rickshaws where a guy holds the two bars and runs through the streets.

We were just two young kids having fun. For a couple of days, we did that. We were nothing more than just innocent friends. It was hard for me to adjust. I just came out of the jungles of Vietnam and now I was with a pretty girl in this big city.

I gave her an address to write to me in Vietnam, and she did. When I got back to the U.S., she continued to write to me for a few months. After that we lost touch. I am sure she is a grandmother now somewhere in Australia.

That was the end of my R & R experience. I really enjoyed it. A couple days later I was back in the jungles with my unit. The two worlds could not have been more different.

Soldiers of the 1st Brigade, 101st Airborne Division in old Viet Cong trenches

Vietnam was full of highs and lows. Days, even weeks, would go by without anything happening, but you would have to be vigilant at all times. That is why every night you were on guard duty. You had to watch where you stepped. As soon as you stopped doing that, something bad would happen.

I was doing guard duty every night between 2:00 and 4:00 in the morning, listening to every little sound. You did not have big battles; it was always an ambush. A tripwire or boobytrap somewhere. The Viet Cong could not sustain a big battle and stay out there and fight. The North Vietnamese would only get you when the odds were in their favor.

We were working with the ROKs, the Republic of Korea soldiers. They were a blocking force and we were pushing an enemy division into them. We had a brigade spread out, maybe three miles long, and for several days we were trying to push the Viet Cong into where the ROKs were.

On the third or fourth day the lead platoon squad ran into an ambush. There was all kinds of firing going on, and I found Captain Moody with three radios. One for artillery, one for the ships offshore, and one to call in airstrikes. There was sustained firing for about fifteen minutes. Several from the lead squad were wounded or killed.

Another squad was sent out to bring the lead squad back and they were ambushed and pinned down. So, there was only one other squad of fifteen men left. We took a high perimeter and Captain Moody started calling in airstrikes.

We had the artillery and planes coming over dropping bombs and napalm. It was happening probably about 100 yards away and it was getting close to dark. One squad was able to make it back carrying several dead soldiers while we formed a perimeter.

I was able to get some more ammo and M16s off the soldiers who were brought back. Then I went and set up several claymores out front. There was this German Shepherd that was running around, his handler had gotten killed.

I grabbed the dog and had him with me all night. I figured he would sniff out any Viet Cong who were around and alert me. I had two M16s, 400 rounds of ammo, several grenades, and claymores set out in front in addition to the German Shepherd. I kept the dog in between my legs, thinking if he sensed anything he would immediately alert me.

I had my head on his shoulder and I fell asleep. I woke up and the dog was asleep! I woke him up and in turn when I fell asleep he would wake me up. It went that way all through the night!

The next day nothing happened. The Viet Cong pulled out and we were able to get out of there. It was amazing what Captain Moody had done. He did not carry a rifle; he just had his radios. He was a dangerous guy with those radios!

Soldiers patrolling a field in Vietnam

We were up in Dak To another time, near the Cambodian border. They had a Special Forces camp there. We went up to pull security and help them out. They had an airport there; it was just a dirt runway where they flew in supplies for the Special Forces. They were next to Cambodia and the Ho Chi Minh trail ran through there so that is where a lot of supplies came.

Our platoon was pulling security on the runway to make sure it would stay operational for the flow of supplies. You have three-man teams that you pull security on. Two- on, four-off, 24/7. During the daytime it was better than at night. At night you set out your tripwires and claymores and built your own hooch (tent). You took your poncho liner and used it to keep dry. It rained every day there during the monsoon season.

There were gullies on each side of the runway. It rained for 24 hours straight and these gullies had become like rushing rivers. I had gotten off my two-hour night shift and hit my buddy in the hooch to take my place. I was soaking wet so I took everything off but my underwear before lying down to sleep under my poncho.

The water was rushing so fast it collapsed the dirt I was sleeping on. The next thing I knew I was under water. I had water in my lungs and I was reaching to grab onto something but nothing was there.

I was grabbing nothing but water and dirt from the side of the gully. I did that for several minutes as I kept popping up to get air. Eventually, I was able to find something to cling onto and pull myself out. I was completely exhausted at this point; I did not even know where I was. I did not want to make any noise because I didn't want to get shot by the Viet Cong, or by my own buddies. I did not know if I was outside the perimeter or not.

I didn't want to get up or make a noise. I actually lay there on my back for three or four hours and was able to get a little sleep. The next morning the sun came up and I got my bearings. I realized I was completely naked. The next thing I noticed was that I was covered in leaches. There must have been at least fifty of them latched onto me.

I did not want to move, I could run into a tripwire or alert the Viet Cong. I eventually got up, though, and was able to find an outpost. I had to give a password, which thankfully

I had. They asked me, "What the hell happened to you?" and I told them. I had to get the leaches off me. The only way to get them off you is to take a lit cigarette and burn the leach with it, then they will let go. It took about an hour to get all the leaches off me.

Soldiers riding on an M-48 tank as the 90mm gun fires during a road sweep

I left Vietnam in December of 1966. I received a Purple Heart for being wounded, run over, and shot in the leg. While in Vietnam I turned 19 years old. I was still a young kid but I reenlisted while I was still there. If you did that, you got to choose where you wanted to go. I wanted to go back home, so I went to Fort Ord, California.

Chapter 3
Back from the Jungle

I flew from Saigon to Seoul, Korea, then to Travis Air Force Base outside of San Francisco. All I had was a duffel bag and my khaki uniform. Within 24 hours I had left Vietnam and was back home on American soil.

My best friend Webbie was going to college at Berkley, University of California. He was in the Delta Tau Delta fraternity. I caught a taxi from Travis Air Force Base to the fraternity house at the University. It was a Friday or Saturday night and they were having a fraternity party.

I remember knocking on the door in my military uniform, carrying a duffel bag. Somebody answered the door and looked at me like, "What the hell are you doing here?" Berkley was the most liberal, anti-war college in the United States. Webbie came up and introduced me to everybody and everything turned out fine. I actually ended up spending a couple of nights there in the fraternity house.

It was strange coming out of the jungles of Vietnam to the Delta Tau Delta House in Berkley. I was able to sleep the whole night without pulling guard duty. I ended up buying a car there. One of Webbie's frat brother's father owned a dealership and he gave me a good deal.

From there, I went to Fort Ord where I was stationed. I had basic training there in 1964, it was a big military base. They knew I had just got back from Vietnam and they had this training center down in Hunter Liggett in the mountains.

They tested new weapons there for war. Things like grenade launchers, automatic weapons and so forth were being developed and redefined. They wanted the Vietnam veterans there because we just came back from battle and knew more about the weapons and the tactics being used. I went out there and fired the weapons. I did that for about a year.

After that, I found myself in Seattle. I had been talking to Sharon since I first met her during my layover to Vietnam in 1966. We had been exchanging letters the whole time and upon my return, we got married in December of 1967.

In January of 1968, I received orders to go to Germany. That is where I really got involved and excelled in wrestling. I went to a place called Bad Kreuznach and that is where my wrestling story really began. I went to this German club in Mainz. At the time, Greco-Roman Wrestling was fairly new in the United States. There weren't any coaches or clubs. The best wrestlers in Freestyle were able to win the National Grecos because they were just better athletes. They cannot do this today. The coaching and the tournaments are better. I was in this German club back then and they had an Olympic Champion and several World Medalists training there.

One of them won a gold medal in the Olympics and three World Medals. His name was Wilfried Dietrich. He was not only coaching there but still competing. In 1972 at the Olympic games in Munich, he wrestled the American heavyweight Chris Taylor. He was the heaviest to ever wrestle in the Olympics, at 6'5" and 450 pounds. Wilfried was outweighed by 200 pounds in this match.

This is where strategy comes into play in wrestling. They were in the Olympic Village in Munich. They had all the athletes there and several mats were spread out where they could warm up and drill. Wilfried did not know if he could actually lock his arms around Chris Taylor because he was so enormous. During one of the practice sessions Wilfried was able to train with Chris Taylor and realized that he could get his hands around his body and lock his fingertips. He knew that he could get that lock. No one had ever thrown Chris Taylor. He was not worried about that because he was so huge.

This is where leverage and technique come into play. During the Olympic match, Wilfried was able to lock his hands and sort of squat underneath his opponent. He pulled Chris Taylor on top of him as he was going back to a high bridge, carried him, and when he got halfway, he hit the mat and turned because he had all of Chris Taylor's weight on him. He then pinned Taylor. It was one of the greatest Olympic throws in history.

I worked with Wilfried Dietrich for about a year and a half at the wrestling club in Mainz. I learned a lot during that time. My technique greatly improved working out with the German club every day.

That is where I was able to excel, especially in Greco. No one in the U.S. had a World Medal in Greco, no one really coached Greco. It was fairly new to the United States. Everybody was wrestling Folkstyle, which is high school collegiate. In that style they attack the legs and have a much lower stance.

In Greco it is more of an erect stance. You wrestle from the waist up. All the techniques have to be from the waist up: headlocks, shoulder throws, arm throws, body locks and such. We did not really have true Greco-Roman wrestlers in the United States at the time. Most of the wrestlers would stay low and attack the legs. They did not develop the skills of Greco. Back then, they had over 200,000

Folkstyle high school and collegiate wrestlers. Greco-Roman had only about 40. That has changed since then, but that was how it was back then.

Getting back to Germany, after the wrestling club in Mainz, I went to Bad Kreuznach. There my job was "Sports Director." That is where my first daughter was born on July 16th, 1969. We named her Wendy Gail Winter.

While in Bad Kreuznach, I had a very unique experience. I had a friend who was a Lieutenant and he set it up that he and I would go to the German Jump School. If you made five jumps with them, they would award you with German Jump Wings. You could wear them on your military uniform.

The Germans had a brigade that would make the jumps and we would jump with them. We stayed with them in their barracks. The winds were so high during the day that we had to jump at night. Sometimes we would jump two times a night. It was a unique experience doing that with the Germans.

They had a Sergeant Major there from the German Airborne Brigade who actually fought in WWII. He had 500 jumps or something like that. He was one tough S.O.B. He was awarded the Iron Cross, which is equivalent to the Medal of Honor in the United States for valor.

At night, the Germans would have beer with their dinner. I had a few beers in me and I asked the German Sergeant Major how he won the Iron Cross. He told me that he had been in Russia, near Stalingrad. There, he had his first battle in hand-to-hand combat with the Russians. He killed them all. I asked him, "Did you shoot them, Sergeant Major?" He replied, "No, I used my trenching tool (a little shovel)." He had killed all of them, rallied his troops, and was able to escape. I thought, "I don't want this Sergeant Major getting mad at me!" I wore those German Wings proudly on my United States Military Uniform until I retired in 1986.

German Jump Wings and various medals

The town of Bad Kreuznach has a special meaning to me because that is where I got started. It is just a beautiful little town. I would drive to Mainz, which was about 45minutes from Bad Kreuznach, to the German Wrestling Club. The coaching was great and they enjoyed having me there. I was able to learn a lot from them. Being in an environment like that really improved my wrestling.

In 1969 they had the Army Championships in Europe. I wrestled in the event and won both the Greco and Freestyle Championships. No one knew who I was… I was just a normal soldier. I actually did quite well, I was able to pin everybody.

I was selected to go back to the Army training camp and wrestle for the Army Team. That is where I met my coach, Ed Steers. I then wrestled in the Armed Forces Championships where the Navy, Army, Marines, and Air Force competed against one another. That is one of the best tournaments in the United States because of the rivalry amongst the services and the talent.

They had the Armed Forces Championships at the Air Force Base in Ohio. I wrestled in those and won the Armed Forces Championships. That qualified me to go to the National Championships.

I could not go, though, because I had to go back to Germany.

I had a baby in Germany and my wife was there and I would be gone another two to three months. I went back there and that summer my wife and daughter flew back to my wife's parents in Seattle. I could not leave until a few months later.

I left Bad Kreuznach in June of 1970 and went back to Fort Bragg. At the time if you were Airborne that was really the only place you could go that had the Airborne division.

Fort Bragg was a wild place back then. You had thousands of veterans from Vietnam there. It was just a wild, wild place. Soldiers came back with PTSD, and when you mix that with alcohol and drugs you get a lot of crazy things going on. It was like *Dodge City*.

When I went back to Fort Bragg my marriage was disintegrating. She wanted me to come back to Seattle, but I did not want to. Everything just started to fall apart, as happens in many marriages. It was basically my fault, being wild at Fort Bragg with guys I knew from back in Vietnam. She wanted me to move back to Seattle and work for her father and I just did not want to do that. So, that was on me but we did have a beautiful daughter together.

Chapter 4
Gold in Turkey

Floyd Winter (2nd from left) with General Askey (middle) (Photo Credit: Steers, Ed)

In 1971 they had the Army Training Camp at Fort Belvoir in Virginia, right outside of Washington D.C., to train for the Armed Forces Championships. So, I went there. I joined the camp because I was still a competitor. I competed all through the 1970s as an athlete and I also coached.

1971 Interservice Freestyle and Greco Team Champions (Photo Credit: Steers, Ed)

One of the reasons I approved of the training camp was because back then they had the draft. It was during the Vietnam era and when your draft letter came you had to enter the Army. Some of the people they drafted were NCAA Wrestling Champions. These athletes would join the camp and I would have a chance to train with them and better my skills. There was a deep talent pool and once again, Ed Steers was the coach.

Ed is an amazing coach. He can tell you who won 3rd place at the NCAA World Championships in 1958. He has a wealth of knowledge.

That year at the Armed Forces Championships I was unable to compete because I cracked a rib training. I could not wrestle because of my injury. I did not get hurt until the very end; it was a great year training with all those NCAA Champions and All Americans.

In 1972 they had another training camp for the Armed Forces Championships. I attended again. Usually January, February and March are when the Armed Forces Championships take place. Then if you qualify for that and win the Armed Forces, you get to go to the Nationals. If you win the Nationals, then you can qualify for the World Team wrestle offs. If you win those, you are on the United States Team, the Olympic Team, or the World Team.

So, Ed Steers was the Army Coach and we went to the Michigan Open, which was one of the better tournaments at the time in the United States. Ed knew every wrestler in the United States. He knew what weight they were at and what they did in high school or college. His brain just worked that way.

He was really big on winning the Team Trophy. He would go look at the line-ups of the teams and decide who was going to win the trophy. He was usually right. At the weigh ins Ed would not let me weigh in, he had me wait. He was adding up the points in his head and he wanted me to wrestle at heavyweight because he said I could beat all those guys.

I finally weighed in and the defending NCAA Heavyweight Champion steps in the door. Ed's face dropped to the floor. He said, "We just lost the Team Trophy." I made it to the finals with the NCAA Heavyweight Champion. I got to the 3rd period and I was actually winning. The time was ticking down, 30 seconds, 20 seconds, and Ed was looking more and more excited. The match ended and I won. They raised my hand and Ed said, "I knew you could do it, Floyd!"

Again, I was doing well in Greco because there were not many Americans who understood Greco. That year in 1972 I won both styles, Freestyle and Greco. That put me on the Armed Forces Team that would wrestle in the World Championships in Turkey. Ed Steers was once again the coach of that team as well.

1972 Interservice Freestyle and Greco Team Champions (Photo Credit: Steers, Ed)

Before leaving for Turkey, I was given the nickname "Bad News." It happened at the New York Athletic Tournament in 1972 in NYC. The backstory is that I had made the finals and they had the pairings on the wall. Bill Farrell was there; he was the coach of the New York AC Club and was also the coach of the 1972 Olympic team that wrestled in Munich where they won six medals. They were one of the most successful wrestling teams ever.

One of his guys was next to him and asked, "Coach, who do I have next?" Farrell said, "You have that guy right there, from the Army." He turned to Farrell and said, "Oh, that's good news." Well, in the finals, I pinned him in 12 seconds. Farrell then told his wrestler, "No, that was bad news." That is how I got the nickname "News" or "Bad News."

After getting my nickname I was on my way to Turkey. We flew from Washington D.C. to Frankfurt, Germany, then on to Istanbul. We had been flying about 20 hours by the time we landed in Istanbul. On the runway in Istanbul an airplane had been hijacked by terrorists. We could see the plane that was being held by the hijackers. It was surrounded by tanks.

This caused a problem for us because we had to get to the match for weigh ins and our plane could not take off. So, the coaches decided we would have to take an overnight train from Istanbul to Ankara. We all got taxis from the airport to the train station, but it was late at night. We could not get a sleeping car on the train so we were put in the dining car. We spent six to seven hours on the train and it was cold, drafty, and uncomfortable. We arrived the next morning.

When we arrived, I was not feeling very well. I could tell I was getting sick. With the jetlag, no sleep, and the drafty dining car, I could feel a cold coming on. We checked into our hotel in Ankara and the next day was weigh ins.

I went to my room and I was feeling terrible. They called a doctor to come over and take a look at me. A Turkish doctor came; he did not speak English, and I did not speak Turkish. He looked at me and took my temperature and this and that. He gave me these pills to take and some eyedrops for my eyes. So, I took those all night. The next morning, I woke up and I felt better. I actually felt pretty good.

I went to weigh ins. There you had about 250 athletes in ten weight classes. You had to weigh in with no clothes on so everyone there was naked. You could wear your skivvies but when you stepped on the scale you had to take them off too. So, I was there and I was putting the eye drops in my eyes. The Turkish doctor I saw the night before was there and he came up to me and was saying something in Turkish. I could not understand him so he got an interpreter. The interpreter explained to me that the drops I was putting in my eyes were supposed to go in my nose! All the people there started laughing. Well, it did not stop me from beating them and getting that gold medal! I wanted to find out where I could get more of those eye drops.

I was the first American to win a gold medal in Greco-Roman in world level competition at the World Military Championships.

An interesting thing happened at this competition as well. There was an ongoing competition between the Iranians and the Turks because wrestling is the number one sport in their countries. They were competing for the Team Title. I was the only American to get a gold medal in Ankara but we also had an American wrestling in the weight class where if the Iranian pinned the American they would win the Team Title.

The Iranians came to the American and tried to get him to throw the match. They would pay him $2,000 or something like that. But he was red, white and blue through and through and told them, "No way, I'm not gonna take any money!" It made him really mad and since he was so fired up, we thought he was going to go out there and kick that guy's butt. However, it did not work out that way and he was pinned and lost the match. Unfortunately, a lot of stuff goes on at the international level, athletes throwing matches and stuff like that.

Floyd Winter (first row, 2nd from rear) and his first CISM (Conseil International du Sport Militaire) Team (Photo Credit: Steers, Ed)

Later on, I actually ended up on the boxing team at Fort Bragg. The Army boxing team was training there full-time and I was in the gym working out doing some neck bridges. The boxing coach came over and said, "You're the wrestler, aren't you?" I said, "Yeah, I am." That year I had won the Armed Forces Championships in both Greco and Freestyle and sometimes people recognized me.

He asked me, "Would you like to box for our team?" I told him, "I don't know anything about boxing." He said, "You'd be on the novice team and I think you would do pretty well."

He told me it would be great conditioning for me. I told him I would give it a shot. So, I started training with the Army Boxing Team. Every day they had a five-mile run, did a lot of stretching for flexibility, crunches, sit-ups, footwork, and stuff like that. I thought it was great, I enjoyed it. They taught me the nuts and bolts of how to box. I actually had a couple of fights.

The big match for Fort Bragg is the Marine Corps from Camp Lejeune. They fight them in a dual match. That year it was at Fort Bragg. The Marine Corps heavyweight was the Armed Forces Champion in boxing. Our heavyweight for the Army got hurt and could not fight.

I only weighed about 195 pounds. But in boxing back then, anything over 177 pounds was a heavyweight. So, the coach came to me and he wanted me to fight. Of course, back then I was young and stupid, so I said, "Yeah, I'll fight, coach." That night the place was packed, they had about a thousand people with music playing from the Army Band.

In the locker room they taped my hands and put Vaseline on me. They were playing James Brown's song "I Feel Good!", trying to fire me up. I said, "I'm ready to go!"

I went out there and my opponent was huge. He was about 6'4" and 240 pounds. Just a mean-looking guy. He was, after all, the Armed Forces Heavyweight Boxing Champion. They announced me as the Armed Forces

Heavyweight Wrestling Champion, not that it mattered. It was not like I could grab him and tie him up. They just wanted to amp up the crowd.

Before the fight started the coach told me to not go straight in…to jab, stick and move, and circle to your right. I said, "Okay, I can do that." I went out there and I was sticking and moving. The next thing I know, I hear the referee counting, "Five, six…" and I am lying down on the canvas.

I got up and blood was running from my mouth. I tied him up after that and ran around for the rest of the period. I went and sat down and they were shoving these gauzes up my nose. The coach told me, "You're lookin' good, Floyd! You're lookin' good! Stick and move! Stick and move!" I said, "Okay" and the second period started.

I walked out there and the next thing I know… I woke up in the locker room! He knocked me out! I went to the hospital that night. When you got knocked out, they had to take you to the hospital for observation. That ended my boxing career! I retired with a record of one win and one loss. I only trained in boxing for a couple of weeks before that fight. If it would have been in wrestling, it would've been a different story.

In 1972 I got out of the Army after eight years of service. I had a couple colleges that offered me scholarships for wrestling and I ended up going back to California. I had been wrestling for three or four years straight by that time. I did not really have the fire to wrestle in college, it was a different style, you had to wrestle collegiate. They did not have Greco or Freestyle.

I liked the coach at USIU so I went there. It was a private school. The school was in San Diego which was a nice city, but I only spent three or four months there. I remember the first class I went to, I wore a coat and tie. I was running a little late and when I walked in the classroom all these 18 and 19-year-old kids saw me and shut up. They went and sat down. They thought I was their teacher!

We stayed in dorms and I had a roommate, he was 18-years-old and I was 26 at the time. It just did not work out. My mind was not into school and wrestling, I was more into having a good time and relaxing.

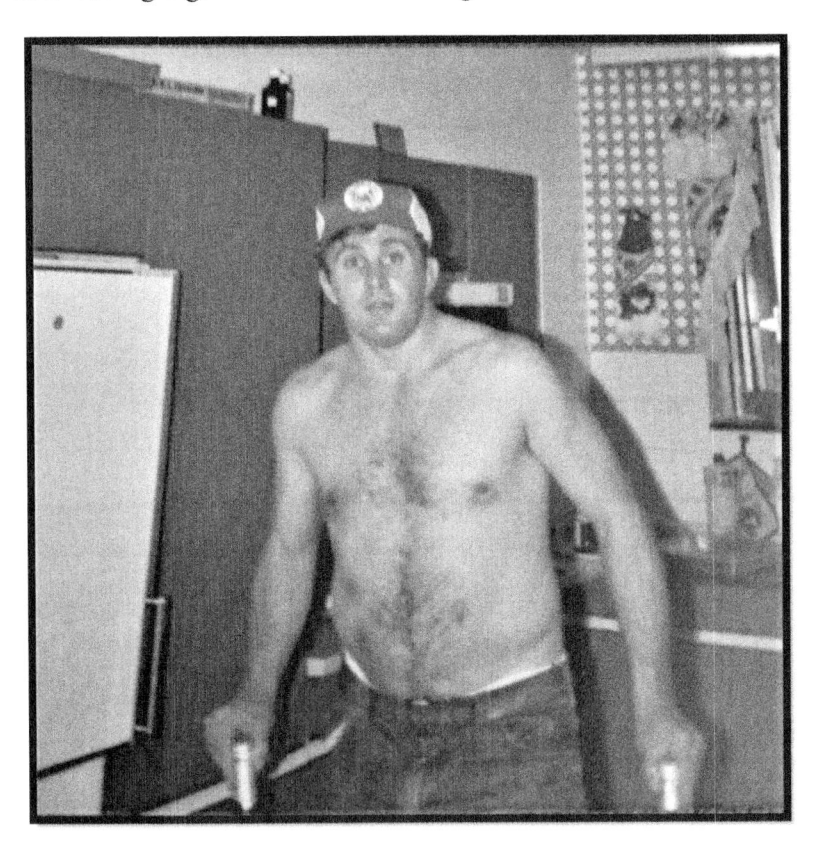

Floyd Winter (Photo Credit: Griffin, Venecom)

I just was not able to adjust to school life. Besides that, I was called in to see the assistant AD and was told the school was having financial problems and would have to take away part of my scholarship. I asked him how much I would have to pay and he said half, which was about $10,000. I could not afford that.

After that I left and headed to San Francisco, where my best friend Webbie was living. He was working there as a bartender and I lived with him for about a year. I worked as a security guard part-time. It was a wasted year but it was fun.

Then in 1974 I decided to go back into the Army. I missed it; I missed the environment. I went and saw a recruiter and had no problems getting back in. My assignment was at West Point. I remember catching the bus from Manhattan to West Point in February in a big snowstorm. They dropped me off at the main gate of West Point.

It was 2:00 AM and I did not know where to go. They took me to this building and put me up for the night.

I was there for about two weeks then went to the Army training camp where they trained the team. That was down in Fort Dix, New Jersey. That same year I won the Armed Forces Championships again.

Floyd Winter winning gold at the Armed Forces Championships

Chapter 5

Love at First Sight

February 7th, 1975, I met my wife Paula. I went to the Officer's Club to get something to eat. I was having a beer after I ate and I noticed this girl sitting at a table. She caught my eye. She was beautiful and I was stunned by her. It was like I ran into a brick wall. Just the way she was laughing and her mannerisms, it was hard for me to take my eyes off her.

I did not want her to think I was stalking her or something, but I was in awe of her. My friend and I began to leave to go back to our dorms. We got out to the parking lot and I told my friend I had to go back in and say something to her. I did not want to leave and miss my opportunity.

When I was walking back into the Officer's Club it was like I was getting ready to wrestle an Iranian in the finals. My stomach was turning. I knew there was a high possibility of getting rejected. I walked up to her table and introduced myself. I told her I was here for a few weeks training and she said, "For what?" and I said, "For wrestling." We made a little small talk.

I told her I noticed her from afar and was very impressed with her smile. Then I asked her for her phone number. She got a piece of paper and wrote it down. I thought maybe it was not her real number and she was just trying to get rid of me. I took the paper and called her the next day and sure enough, it was her.

Floyd and Paula Winter, June 21, 1975

A couple days later I went over to where she lived and brought her some flowers. We talked and had dinner that weekend. Four months later we decided to get married.

We flew to Las Vegas in June and it was smokin' hot there. Even at night it was over 100 degrees. We went to the city hall to get our marriage license. There was a line of about 20 couples waiting to get their marriage licenses.

We were in line and I realized I recognized the girl in front of us. I said to myself, "I know her from somewhere." It turned out to be Cher! Cher and Gregg Allman. They were in line to get their marriage license too. I said, "Aren't you Cher?" She said, "Yeah!" And we talked for a few minutes about getting married. Cher ended up getting divorced soon after. Later, I remember telling Paula, "Well, we lasted longer than they did!"

We got our marriage license and that same day we had to be at the chapel. In Vegas you can get anything you want for your wedding. You can get people to cry for you, throw rice, whatever. I was going to pay for them to say, "That groom is a very good-looking guy!" I was nervous, had a dry mouth, and Paula was nervous too. We got married and it only took about ten minutes.

After getting married a lot of people fly to Europe or some exotic place for their honeymoon. What we did was a little bit different. We walked over to the A&W root beer stand and had a root beer.

When Paula and I got married she had a previous son named Paul. He was seven when we got married and I adopted him.

That was forty-five years ago and she has been my coach through all those years. She is a wonderful mother. With my job I had to travel all over the world and she had to stay home with the kids. I was able to take her on some of the trips I went on, but she usually had to stay back with the children.

After getting married in Las Vegas, we went back to West Point and got a little cottage in Cornwall. It is about seven miles from West Point over the mountain. We lived there for about a year and a half. At that time, I was still wrestling and while I was there I helped out with training the cadets from West Point.

So, I was the Assistant Coach at West Point while I was still wrestling for the Army team. My son Jason was born there in 1976. I spent three years at West Point until 1977, when I was assigned to Berlin, Germany.

Floyd Winter holding his son Jason (Photo Credit: Griffin, Venecom)

I had to go ahead of my wife to Berlin and she came a little while later with the baby. I had to find a place to live and get oriented before they could come. At the time they still had the wall up around the city. Our apartment was about half a mile from the wall.

That is where I met General Moore. He was the Commander of the Berlin Brigade.

While I was there, I wrestled for a German Club in the Bundesliga. It was a German league where you would wrestle matches around the country. You would fly down to West Germany, Munich, Frankfurt, wherever, and wrestle different clubs.

The Germans were allowed two foreigners on a team and it was me and a Turk. I would drive down to their club two or three days a week.

The three years we spent in Berlin were a fun time. I also got involved with the Turkish club there. They had 100,000 Turks who lived in Berlin and wrestling was a popular sport among them. A Turkish club asked me to wrestle for them and I did. That was a way I made some good friends with the Turks.

The Turks I wrestled with did not have any showers in their wrestling facilities. I would wrestle for two to three hours and be drenched in sweat, smelling. Paula would not let me into our apartment after training. She made me strip down and take off all my clothes because I stunk so bad.

The Turkish ambassador for Germany invited me over to his house for dinner. He gave me this gift of a huge, fragile, glass mosque. Unfortunately, when it was shipped back to the States, it got broken.

Floyd Winter (right) with a Turkish wrestler (Photo Credit: Griffin, Venecom)

The Winter family with a Turkish wrestler in Berlin, Germany (Photo Credit: Griffin, Venecom)

I ended up starting a Berlin wrestling club for our soldiers. I was able to get a couple of guys from the Army Wrestling Team to be stationed in Berlin. We had try outs and a club was formed.

Berlin Wrestling Team (Photo Credit: Griffin, Venecom)

I was able to get them off two days a week just to train for wrestling. During the wrestling season for the Army they had tournaments in West Germany at different military installations. You had to take the duty train overnight to wrestle and then take the duty train back.

Floyd Winter on the duty train in Berlin, Germany (Photo Credit: Griffin, Venecom)

We had a really good team. We had time to train and great coaching. General Moore gave us the opportunity to do this. He allowed us to train and travel for matches.

General William C. Moore was at the Pentagon and the Army Chief of Staff, who was a Four-Star General, called him in. He said, "We need your help, William. I am going to send you to take over the Berlin Brigade."

They were surrounded by the wall and the Russians in Berlin. They had the American Army, the British, and the French there surrounded by the wall. The Four-Star General at the Pentagon told General Moore that we really need your help.

What had happened was that a lot of soldiers in the Berlin Brigade were getting intoxicated and arrested for fighting. General Moore looked to me to turn things around. What I was doing with the wrestling team seemed to have a positive impact on the soldiers. Instead of a soldier getting arrested for a DUI and fighting, Berlin Brigade won another tournament.

He let me train the team the way I wanted to. I was not only the Head Coach, I also actively wrestled and competed. I took them to Denmark to wrestle the Danish National Team and various other places. General Moore gave me the freedom to take these soldiers and go to these different countries to do these international tournaments.

I was one of the first Greco athletes and coaches in the Army because I had the experience from wrestling in Mainz with the Olympic Champion, Coach Wilfried Dietrich. That experience helped me to earn 14 gold medals in the Armed Forces Championships. As a coach I was able to develop athletes at that high, high level.

I really created my own job in the Army because there was no place for me. I had an MOS job description but there was no one at that level who coached the Army and the Armed Forces, and was a National Coach, Olympic Coach etc. I was the head of a world-class program that I had built from the ground up. It was not so much even for my coaching ability. I was able to use the position to write letters to generals to get some of my people out of their military assignments to come and wrestle. When I retired from the Army, my job title was retired as well. I was the only one to ever hold that position.

DEPARTMENT OF THE ARMY
UNITED STATES MILITARY ACADEMY
WEST POINT, NEW YORK 10996

MARS-Y   16 October 1984

Director
Combat Development
Ft Rucker, AL 36362

1. All too often people are so busy in their own pursuits they seldom find or take time to reflect upon those in other areas that touch many of us favorably. You have such a person in your command.

2. I speak of CPT Gary Barber. As a member of the 1984 Army wrestling team, CPT Barber was second in the interservice wrestling championships and third in the national wrestling championships. CPT Barber was selected as a member of the United States team to compete in the World Cup Championships, 6-8 Oct in Caracas, Venezuela, but was unable to go because of his military duties.

3. The Army wrestling team won the 1984 national championships party due to CPT Barber's wrestling skills, expertise and team spirit, which contributed greatly to the successful performance of the team. I have the highest respect and admiration for him. He has that special type of courage that permits him to ignore pain and adversity. He competed this year with a severely separated shoulder.

4. In addition to his wrestling, CPT Barber has represented the United States Army while conducting various wrestling clinics at many high schools. Based on his skill and ability to relate to these students, these clinics were highly successful and gave a great boost to the Army recruiting efforts.

5. CPT Barber is not only an outstanding officer, but is one of the best wrestlers in the United States. He has a good chance of being national champion and world medalist if he is afforded the opportunity to train and participate in national and international competitions.

6. The laurels and national recognition CPT Barber received continues to be a source of pride for the Army and contributes favorably to our public image. His untiring dedication to excellence and his unique ability as a soldier athlete reflects great credit upon your command and the Army.

MARS-Y   16 October 1984

7. My intention is to give a humble person, who normally would go unnoticed among you, his proper credit. I would be remiss in my duties as Army Wrestling Coach, member of the national coaching staff and as the Assistant Olympic Wrestling Coach, if I did not bring this to your attention.

                                        Floyd Winter

                                        SFC FLOYD N. WINTER
                                        Army Wrestling Coach

A letter from Floyd Winter for his solider-wrestler Gary "Big Hands" Barber

While in Germany we hosted the International Friendship Cup, which was with the Turkish Team, German Team, Dane Team, and us, the Americans. The ambassadors for those countries also came to the event. Many high-level officials attended and it was an incredibly positive experience for everyone involved.

For the Danish tournament we got a vehicle and drove to Denmark and wrestled in a big sports hall there.

It was a very good match, they had about 1,500 people in attendance. At the end they gave us this beautiful glass trophy. When I got back to Berlin, I gave it to General Moore. He really liked it and put it with his other awards in his office.

We trained during the day and I would go to a Turk or German club in the evening. I was a full-time wrestler and coach. That was my job in Berlin.

I hosted the Freedom Cup Championships in Berlin and invited the Turks, Germans, and Danes. I marketed it and the generals and ambassadors from those countries came to the match. We had an opening ceremony, music, and awards. It turned out to be a really nice event. General Moore attended the event and really enjoyed it.

Later on in life I would meet General Moore in Washington, D.C. for dinner. He told me that I had really done a lot to help him after he was sent to Berlin by the Army Chief of Staff. He said, "You really saved my bacon." General Moore had been sent to Berlin to straighten out the mess the soldiers were causing by being intoxicated and getting into drunken brawls. There were four countries there at the time and the United States did not need any bad publicity. It was embarrassing for America.

General Moore told me, "When I got to Berlin, I didn't really know how I was going to do it. You really helped me out by having this team, all the positive things that came from it, the VIPs and different countries that attended the events." He said it helped him a lot that there were positive stories in the paper every week instead of the bad publicity that was happening before.

While in Berlin, I would go back every year to the Army Team to wrestle and take part in the Armed Forces Championships.

Chapter 6
Stay Low and Circle Left

1978 was a busy year for me. I made the team to go to the World Military Championships in Tehran, Iran. That was when my daughter Jennifer was born as well, at West Point.

I was back in the U.S. for the Armed Forces Championships and they were in Quantico, Virginia, at the Marine Base. Paula was still pregnant with Jennifer at the time, actually she was two or three weeks overdue.

Paula came down to see me wrestle but she was struggling. She could barely walk or get out of a chair. I was in the finals against a Marine. It came down to the last 30 seconds and the score was tied. We were both pummeling and pushing and trying to pull out the victory.

Paula had always been my biggest cheerleader. Out of nowhere, my wife who was two to three weeks overdue, jumped up out of her seat and started screaming and yelling at the top of her lungs for me to win! She was going wild jumping up and down!

The referee was Rick Tucci. The rules were they would caution somebody out for stalling. They stopped the match, cautioned the Marine out and I won. The referee told me later, "Floyd, I had to stop that match because your wife Paula was going to have that baby right there on the mat!" Because of my wife I won the gold medal. I told her if she could stay pregnant until the summer for the Olympic and World Team trials that would be great. She of course said, "No way!"

We went back to West Point and as soon as we got back we went to the hospital. The doctor told us the baby would not be coming for a day or two. The doctor said I could go and they would call me if anything happened. So, I went back to the dorm where I was staying. I heard a bang on the door around 2:00 AM and I was told the baby is coming now!

I got in the car and rushed over to the hospital. I parked in front and ran up to the 2nd floor. They saw me running down the hall and were screaming to hurry up because the baby was coming. They gave me these slip-ons to put over your shoes and a cap to put over your hair. So, I am running, putting these things on my shoes and the cap on my head. As soon as I ran into the delivery room Jennifer was being born.

The nurse and doctors looked at me and said, "What the hell do you have on?" What I did was put the cap on my shoe and those shoe things on my head! I looked like an idiot! Later on, I told Jennifer the story and apologized for embarrassing her when she was born.

After she was born I had to go to the World Championships in Tehran, Iran. For security reasons they did not put us up in a hotel in downtown Tehran. This was six months before the Iran hostage crisis at the U.S. Embassy. They put us in an Iranian military base outside the city. It took us about an hour to get to their stadium every morning.

They have a stadium dedicated only to wrestling that seated about 20,000 people. They had a big throne at the top where the Shah would sit. He never did come to the match but his brother who was a Lieutenant General Chief of Staff of the Iranian Army was there. The stadium was completely packed every night!

That was probably one of the worst trips I have ever been on. The accommodations were so bad, they were terrible. Of course, as an athlete you have to hydrate and eat properly. Once we left on the bus that morning to go to the wrestling facility, we were there all day. We were trapped there.

They did not provide anything. Whatever we had we brought from our morning breakfast. They did not give us food, water, or anything at the stadium all day long. We would return to the Iranian military base late at night. They had some food but I could not even tell what it was. You did not even know what you were eating. It looked like grease.

I would have weigh ins soon and I was about two pounds over. I put on some sweats and was going to go for a two to three mile run in the scorching Iranian heat to drop the pounds. I went outside the military gate and started running in the desert.

As I was running, I saw fresh dirt dug up in front of me. I was running by it when I looked and saw this hole. Before I knew it, this thing jumped out of this hole right into my chest!

It was a wild dog, a mother protecting her puppies. The thing jumped on me and was snarling and snapping at me. What should have been a ten-minute run back to the Iranian base only took me two! Anyway, I lost the weight I needed to make weigh ins and wrestle.

The next day was weigh ins and the wrestling started that day. I was the only American to make it to the finals. The Iranians would put their best wrestlers in the military just so that they could be at this event. The event was televised all over Iran. They wanted Iranians to see the Americans getting beat up.

It was no surprise I got sick over there. The food was bad, the water was bad, and I was severely dehydrated. I felt horrible. That happens when you are in some of these third world countries. I ended up losing eight or nine pounds from being sick.

It was the finals and I was in a tunnel in the Iranian stadium. The Iranians were cheering and going crazy. They had seven wrestlers in the finals and they were beating everybody up.

They had a loud horn in the stadium. Someone would get on the loud horn and go…do-ta-do…Iran! Then the entire stadium of 20,000 people would say, "Iran!" The crowd would go wild. Then someone on the loud horn would say, "Ali Ali Akbar (God is Great)!" The crowd would repeat the phrase and go wild, waving their Iranian flags.

So, I was in the tunnel in the stadium watching and listening to all of this. I have to admit, it was quite intimidating. Then I heard my name over the loud horn, "Floyd Winter, USA!"

We walked out of the tunnel to the middle of the stadium where they had a raised mat. All the Iranian television cameras were on me. I got to the mat and walked up the stairs. My opponent came out of another tunnel being carried on the shoulders of his comrades. They were screaming, "Ali Ali Akbar!"

He came to the mat, we shook hands, they blew the whistle and we started to wrestle. In the first 20 seconds of the match the Iranian got a takedown on me on the edge of the mat. He then punched me in the face and my eye closed. They stopped the match. They had this Iranian trainer run up to me with a spray bottle of alcohol or something. He then sprayed the stuff in my face!

It got in my eyes and I could not see! He also sprayed it in my mouth, making it hard for me to breathe. I was doing everything I could to just get this guy away from me. I knew that because I was in Iran the referee was not going to help me out. The Iranian wrestler could have shot me with a gun or stabbed me with a knife and they would not have called a foul.

The Iranian crowd was in a frenzy now. I got up and shook it off and kept going. There was a flurry on the edge of the mat again. My opponent did an Iranian single leg on me where he got in high on my thigh and picked me up and swept back. I landed on my shoulder and I heard a crunch. Of course, it was injury time again and the Iranian trainer came running out spraying me all over with alcohol.

I got up and had a hard time lifting my shoulder. My eye was swollen shut and I was really pissed off now. I actually got a takedown on him, but I could not turn him so they put us back up. Then I attacked again and had a low single but he took his leg and kneed me right in my face, breaking my nose.

The blood immediately started gushing out. Here comes the Iranian trainer again with his spray bottle of alcohol. My eye is closed, my shoulder is sagging, and now my nose is broken and it is still the first period.

The period ends and I go sit down. I am waiting for my coach to tell me what to do to motivate me and lead me to victory. I need his advice and encouragement. The coach comes over and my eye is closed and they are sticking swabs up my nose to stop the bleeding. He looks at me and says, "God, Winter, you look bad!" I could hear the crowd chanting, "Ali Ali Akbar! Iran!" and see them waving their flags. The cameras were coming up and zooming in on me.

I told the coach, "Yeah, I know I look bad, but what should I do against this monster?" He tells me, "Stay low and circle left." I said, "What does that mean, coach?" He said, "If you stay low and circle left, you will be closer to the exit, and can get the hell out of here!"

I lost the match. That night they had a banquet but I could not go because I was so sore and beat up. The next day we were leaving Tehran to fly back to the United States. They had the lights off and I was trying to get some sleep.

The next thing I know, the light comes on. I am thinking, "What the hell?" I look over and at the door is the same Iranian who beat me up. I was wondering, "What the hell is he doing here?"

I didn't know it, but after having a match it is customary for Iranians to exchange gifts. He was about the same size as me so he wanted some of my clothes. At the time they liked our blue jeans. I could not even move so he swung open my suitcase and was picking out clothes.

The next morning, I got up to leave and I had no clothes. I had no pants to wear. It turned out, he left his warmup suit and jewelry in exchange. I put his warmup on, which smelled like hell, but I did not care and left. That was my last vivid memory of Iran.

In 1978 I also had the World Team trials up at Lake Tahoe. I should have made that team. Out of four matches I scored 30 technical points and the other guy only scored 4. The coach was really biased. I was 31 years old at the time. My opponent was 23. He had placed fourth in the World Championships.

I actually won the third match, but then they wanted to see another match. You cannot do that today. A win is a win. So, I had to wrestle him again. Even though at the time I was ahead by six or seven points. The guy was a big bruiser and he kept pushing, and they cautioned me out for stalling. It was bullshit but I went to the World Championships as an alternate in 1978.

They did not have the structure back then that they do now. One guy was in charge of the wrestling. It was easy for him to be biased and pick his favorites. The guy who took my spot in Mexico City at the 1978 World Championships lost his first two matches and ended up not doing very well.

Chapter 7
The Full-Time Coach

Floyd Winter (left) coaching his wrestler in Germany (Photo Credit: Griffin, Venecom)

In 1979 the European Championships were held in Berlin. I was not there, I got selected for some other assignments and went back to the States. In 1980 the Military European Championships were held in Italy.

I was back in Germany and we had to take a 16-hour bus ride to Italy. We arrived at night and the next day was the weigh ins. After a 16-hour bus ride we wanted to go for a run but they would not let us because it was a secure base. That made me kind of upset. I ended up winning the Championships there anyway.

Army Wrestling Team-Day playing softball (Photo Credit: Cuneo, Ted)

The Commanding General
Marine Corps Development and Education Command
requests the pleasure of your company
at the
Interservice Wrestling Championship Banquet
to be held
Thursday evening, the 25th of March 1982
Diamond Hall
Refreshments at six o'clock
Dinner at seven o'clock
Attire
Civilian, Informal (coat & tie)
Military, Class A Uniform

(Photo Credit: Cuneo, Ted)

I went back to Berlin to spend time with Paula and the kids. I had been away a lot. I wanted to spend time with my children and help Paula out. We left Germany and went back to West Point.

Paula had always wanted to be a flight attendant. That was one of the things she wanted to do in life. We were in West Point at the time and they had job interviews in Boston. That is about four hours from West Point. I went with her to the interview.

Back then you actually had to make a weight standard. She was like three pounds over. She had to lose some weight before the next weigh in and she was with the right guy. I know how to lose weight quickly!

I went to the shower and turned the hot water on. I got the plastic bags that your dry cleaning comes in from the hotel. I put a couple sweatshirts over her and then the plastic. I then turned the steam up from the shower. I kept her in there for about an hour.

The next day she made weight. She got the interview but she did not end up getting the job. I was really shocked because she had all the skills and talent. I don't know why she didn't get the job; she should have. A few years later she applied again and this time got the job as a flight attendant.

She had to go to Chicago for three weeks of training on how to be a flight attendant. I was in West Point while she went to Chicago. She graduated and got assigned to fly out of JFK airport in New York.

She did not know how to get to JFK from West Point yet so I drove her there and picked her up when her flight returned on her first day. I did not get any sleep and got back just in time to take a shower and go to work! She learned how to make the trip on her own eventually and would make the long commute by herself.

Getting back to my career in the military, the Armed Forces instructor asked if I would be the Army Wrestling Coach. I said yes and that ended my wrestling career. I would take on the full-time duties of coaching the Army Team. I was the Head Coach of the Army Team for the next eight years.

We had the Army Training Camp at West Point in 1981 and I was the Head Coach. My former coach Ed Steers became the Head Coach for West Point that same year also. For me, it was a lot of responsibility compared to before. Before I coached and just looked after myself. Now I was solely responsible for 20 to 25 guys. More than half were officers on the team.

I was the only one in the Army who was the supervisor for these officers. I was the boss. I did not want to lead by fear even though I had the power to send them home. I wanted to motivate them to be the best they could be. Every day I wanted them to look in the mirror and ask themselves, "Did I do everything I could today to become better?"

I knew from experience that you had to be in better shape than everyone you wrestle if you expect to win. Conditioning is a very important part of wrestling. I tried to get them in shape and motivate them to feel good about themselves. I believed that this enhanced their chances of winning.

As I stated before, the Armed Forces Championships are one of the best tournaments in the United States because of the talent and the great rivalry among the services. Now, the Army has the WCAP (World Class Athletic Program). They train in Colorado Springs and they have money and are structured like a company. They have a commander and first sergeant. The Army has now won numerous National Championships, fifteen I believe. They have also won the last 21 Armed Forces Tournaments.

When I was the Head Coach we did not have a world-class program. I was basically responsible for everything. I decided where we would go. I borrowed whatever money I could from the Department of the Army. I would try to convince the Army Sports Director that we needed to go to this tournament or send somebody here or there. Of course, he would always say, "No, we don't have the money."

General Scott, Ted Cuneo, and Floyd Winter (left to right) at West Point

He was big into boxing. He was on the Olympic Boxing Committee. His first love was not wrestling. He did not really care if we got gold medals or not. You cannot improve unless you go to tournaments and wrestle someone better.

The Army Sports Director's name was Billy Dove. I would call him up and say, "We need to go to the Michigan Open, Billy." He would respond, "We don't have the money!" Finally, I learned my lesson. I would call him up and say, "Billy, I heard that one of your boxers did a great job!" He would respond, "Oh yeah! He did this and that and won this fight." He would be in a good mood and then I would hit him up for money!

Things have changed now with the WCAP and it is not like that anymore. The money is there.

It is not popular to go into the military when you are at war, and we have been at war for a long time. It is not popular to join the Army, the parents especially do not like it. If you are in the WCAP, basically you just wrestle and compete for the Army Team. If you go to the Nationals, make the World Team, or Olympic Team, they announce, "Private so and so from the Army" and you could not buy positive publicity for the Army like that. The Army gets a lot back for investing in the WCAP.

The United States Recruiting Command is able to utilize this. I did this for about twelve years. I would go to high schools around the country and do clinics for their wrestling teams. The coaches really enjoyed it because you had National Champions from the Army out there doing clinics for their teams.

Interservice Opening Ceremony (Photo Credit: Cuneo, Ted)

If you did this on your own it would cost the high schools several hundred dollars. The Army Recruiting Command got a lot of publicity that they really could not buy this way. I actually did that all through the 1980s. The Recruiting Command would call and ask me if I could get some wrestlers together to go out to these schools. They would cut the orders and give us the funds to do this.

In 1981 I hooked up with a coach by the name of Bill Martel for the Concord Cup in California. He was the Head Coach at the University of California in Berkley. He was on the National Coaching Staff. He founded the Concord Cup and numerous teams from all around the world would come there to compete. I brought the Army Team to wrestle there several times throughout the 1980s.

It was a great opportunity for the American wrestlers to gain experience because you did not have to spend money going overseas. Wrestling teams from all over the world would come here to the United States. They got to wrestle and train with all these Olympic and World Medalists from other countries right here at home.

We set up these dual matches around California. They would go to Stockton or Davis and it would be USA Wrestling vs. Sweden or whatever country was there. I believe Bill Martel did more for Greco with this tournament than anybody else in the United States. He got some money from USA Wrestling for doing it, but it did not cover the hotels, transportation, dining facilities, venue, and to have 30 to 40 staff members to make it all happen.

I got involved with it when I went out there for the Army Team. Randy Couture developed out there too along with Tony Thomas. They would wrestle Olympic Medalists from around the world and train with them. They would greatly improve this way. Bill Martel should be in the Hall of Fame for USA Wrestling for what he accomplished.

Floyd Winter with Tony Thomas after he won the National Championship (Photo Credit: Thomas, Tony)

In 1982 the Army Training Camp was at Fort Bliss, Texas. Throughout the year we would continue to do clinics for the Recruiting Command in different States around the country in the high schools. We had numerous athletes make the Pan American Teams and World Championships. They would go to different tournaments in Europe to wrestle. I was also put on the National Coaching Staff for USA Wrestling. The Army Team had one of the best Greco teams in the United States.

Jimmy Diehl was with me at the training camp at Fort Bliss. The night before a couple of guys got drunk and came in and broke a window or something. I got called on the carpet for that. It was not good because we were there for training and the guys got drunk and broke something.

I asked my guys who did it and no one would say anything. That morning we went to the track and I had them run for about an hour and a half doing sprints. They only had 20 seconds between breaks. Then we went in and I made them do four matches. In the afternoon we had another four or five matches.

That night I went by their rooms and Jimmy Diehl was lying in bed and had the sheet up to his chin. He could not move. He said, "Coach, today you opened a can of whoop ass!"

It had happened the night before and I found out who did it. Of course, they were still hung over and they never did that again.

In 1983 we had Lou Banach on the team; he wrestled at Iowa. He had a twin brother, Ed Banach. Ed won three NCAA titles and Lou won two. They wrestled for Dan Gable out in Iowa. Lou was ROTC and came in the Army for two years. He was on the Army Team. I got him stationed at West Point where he worked out with the cadets. He didn't wrestle Greco; he was specifically Freestyle to make the Olympic Team. He won a gold medal in the Olympics in L.A. His brother also won a gold in L.A. In Freestyle, the U.S. won six medals.

In 1983 we also had the World Military Championships in Caracas, Venezuela. I was the coach of that team. Our wrestler Chris Pease won the gold medal there. Our team won the Team Title and we had numerous medals won.

Chris Pease, 1982 (Photo Credit: Cuneo, Ted)

Chris Pease throwing a dummy (Photo Credit: Cuneo, Ted)

Ted Cuneo (top) and Chris Pease (bottom) wrestling (Photo Credit: Cuneo, Ted)

The Eastern Bloc countries boycotted the Olympics in 1984. Of course, the Eastern Bloc countries had the best wrestlers and they did not come. That would have definitely changed the colors of our medals. In 1980 the Soviets invaded Afghanistan and we had boycotted the Olympics and did not send our teams. So, the Russians paid us back by boycotting the 1984 Olympics. It was all political.

I was selected to be the Assistant Olympic Coach in Los Angeles. Bill Martel was one of the assistant coaches as well. Of course, they had the Armed Forces Championships, the Nationals, and the Olympic Trials. If you win those then you are on the Olympic Team.

We had the training camp for Greco and Freestyle up at Big Bear. It was above L.A. in the San Bernardino mountains. The altitude is about a mile high there, so we chose that spot for the conditioning. It was during the summer and school was out so the Greco Team was using the junior high school and the Freestyle Team was using the high school.

Every morning around 6:00 AM the Greco side of the house would get up. I was in charge of two weight classes, heavyweight and 220 pounds. I was responsible to make sure they got up, took care of their injuries, and looked after their needs and wants. I would also help them in their areas of weakness and things like that.

Our heavyweight was Jeff Blatnick. I would go wake him up at about a quarter to six. The track was right down the road where we would stretch and start doing our wind sprints.

He was a typical heavyweight. After waking him up he would tell me, "Well, coach, my shoulder hurts and I won't be able to do sprints today." He had his excuses and I would turn the radio up full blast and shake the bed to get him up.

I would get him down to the track and make him run. I would force him to do a lot more than he wanted or thought he could do. Sometimes I would wake him up and he would say, "Coach, I don't feel good, I don't think I can do this." I would pull the blankets off him and make him get up.

One time he said, "I can't go." So, I poured water over him while he was still in bed. He chased me out of the room! It is a good thing he didn't catch me or I probably wouldn't be here today.

Eventually I got him down to the track and made him run. I knew at heavyweight if you are in better shape than all the other heavyweights you wrestled, there is a good chance you would win. Especially in the 3rd period, which is what it usually comes down to for the big guys. So, I made him work.

At the Olympic Games he made it to the finals. He was wrestling a Swedish wrestler by the name of Johanson, who had been a World Champ before. He was a big guy who outweighed Jeff by about 40 pounds. The Swede was 280 pounds and Jeff was about 240 pounds.

During the match there were three periods, three minutes each. It came down to the last 30 seconds and it was tied 2–2. They were fighting and I could tell Johanson was dying out there. His legs were wobbling, he was taking deep breaths, and he was leaning into his opponent. Jeff out-pummeled him and beat him to the mat and scored two points.

Floyd Winter at the Los Angeles Olympic Games, 1984

Time ran out and Jeff won the gold medal because of his conditioning. He was ecstatic when they raised his hand on the mat while the crowd of 20,000 people raised American flags and chanted, "USA! USA!" I stayed away from him because it was his time to shine. I was walking back to the locker room when he came and found me. He picked me up off the floor and said, "Coach, thanks for getting me up!"

Years after that he ended up doing a lot of announcing for MMA tournaments and NCAA wrestling. Whenever he saw me at an event or in a restaurant, he would pick me up off the ground and say, "Thanks, coach!" I would always tell him, "That is what a coach does."

Unfortunately, he died six or seven years ago during a surgery.

My hometown, Porterville, is about three hours north of Los Angeles. My family and I got a chance to go see my parents after the Olympics. My friends from high school and I went backpacking into the Sierra mountains. We had pack horses carry all our supplies in. It was 20 miles up and down the mountains. We stayed there for five nights by a river. We would catch fish during the day and camp out at night.

I remember the first night my friend Jeff said we better take our food and put it up in the trees so the bears would not get it. I was not even thinking about bears getting our food or us! We put our food in a duffel bag, tied a rope to it and threw it around a limb. We hauled it up about 25 or 30 feet off the ground.

The next morning around 5:30 AM my friend woke up and said, "You better come out, the bear got into our food!" We went out and the duffel bag was on the ground and the food was scattered all around. The bear had gotten most of our food.

The next day we were able to catch fish and we had some food left. That night we strung it up and put a rope from one tree to another. The bear was able to climb the tree the night before and get our food so we thought this new tactic might work. We did not think he could get the food strung between two trees. The next day the duffel bag was down again and this time all our food was gone!

At this point we were pretty pissed off. We had brought three cases of beer up there with us. It was ice cold because we put it in the river. The next day we caught several trout from the river. We decided it was best to make peace with the bear so we left him a six pack of beer and some trout. The next morning the trout were gone and the beer cans were pierced open.

After that, my family and I drove from California back to West Point in New York. We took our time. It took us four or five days. I went back and helped coach the cadets at West Point while I was still the Army Head Coach. I was also a National Coach, did clinics, and went to Europe two or three times a year. It was definitely a full-time career.

I hardly ever wore my Army uniform. I did not wear it while coaching or going to tournaments. It was not because I did not want to, it was just the circumstances. I had several awards through the military: three Meritorious Service Medals, Vietnamese Cross of Gallantry, Army Commendation Medals, Combat Infantry Badge, Parachute Badge, and German Jump Wings.

I was able to use my unique position in the U.S. Army to get soldiers out of assignments to wrestle. I would write letters to Generals and high-ranking officials to have these soldiers released. It was not something that was given to these soldiers, they had to earn it.

They were expected to go out there and represent the United States, the Army, and their Unit. I wanted to give them the best opportunity I could. You do not send a soldier into battle without any ammo. If it happens that they win a gold medal or place in the Worlds it not only reflects back on that soldier but their Unit and the Army as a whole.

I had a wrestler on the team who I believe was in the class of 1980–81 at West Point. While I was there, he got into trouble. Before you competed against another school you had to show up and be in uniform. They had an inspection before you got on the bus.

They had an Officer in Charge who was responsible for the team. This soldier got in trouble because he was told not to go and wrestle. He took his personal leave and went anyway. He showed up on his own, he was on leave, he was not AWOL or anything. He wrestled and won the tournament.

The Officer in Charge brought him up on charges and they were going to kick him out of West Point. I thought the Officer in Charge overdid it. They were going to throw this guy out for wrestling while he was on leave.

I came to his proceeding, which was similar to a court-martial, and said some words on his behalf. I went in my uniform with my combat badges. They asked me if I would serve in combat with this soldier. I said, "Absolutely, I would serve in combat with him." I told them how I felt about him.

I believed that he should have the opportunity to stay and get his commission at West Point. They did not tell me, but years later I learned that because of that they did not kick him out. He received a punishment but they did not kick him out. He went on and graduated and retired a Colonel in the Army.

Sometimes you get lost in the shuffle. They did not have to do all that with him. I was there to put a stop to it. They probably would have discharged him if I did not go to bat for him.

The bonds that these wrestlers created with one another and myself were incredible. They shared the pain in training, the wins, the losses, the highs, the lows…all in a military training environment. Many became like brothers and decades later these bonds are still as strong as ever.

1985 Interservice Championships (Photo Credit: Thomas, Tony)

An example would be Randy Couture. Randy went on to become a numerous time MMA World Champion and famous movie star. He is still close with many people from the Army Team he was a part of.

One is Ken Popelka. He moved to Las Vegas where Randy was living. Ken should have made the Olympic Team in 1988, but he was robbed from making the team. That is a whole other story. However, at his match in the Armed Forces he beat Buddy Lee. He was a previous Olympian. He beat him in the finals and because of his win, we won the Team Title.

Ken was a State Champion from Wisconsin. Randy has a lot of compassion and love for those guys, including Ken.

Randy called me up and said, "Coach, you better come out here. Ken has been diagnosed with cancer and I don't know how much longer he has." I immediately flew out to Las Vegas. Randy picked me up from the airport and I stayed with him.

The next day we went and picked Ken up and went out to breakfast. We spent three hours there just talking. I could tell I was cheering him up, so that made me happy.

Randy has a gym in Las Vegas and we all went there. Randy has free fitness classes for veterans and he had me give a motivational speech. Randy raises a lot of money each year for veterans by giving speeches, doing motorcycle rides, things like that. He really cares about the military and the veterans.

He goes out to Walter Reed every year. He has really done a lot for the veterans and wounded warriors.

After the gym Kenny gave me a hug and thanked me for coming out. I left and four days later Randy called me again. He said, "Coach, you better come back out, I don't think he's going to make it."

I flew out again, this time with my wife Paula. Randy picked us up from the airport. Randy was going to do a celebration of life for Ken at his house. He invited all the past Army wrestlers to come.

It was a big catered event that cost Randy a lot of money. The event was to happen the next day.

Paula and I were having dinner when Randy called and said, "He passed away." It happened three or four years ago, but I still get choked up over it.

He was such a tough guy. I actually got the film of him wrestling in his high school State Tournament and winning it. I was going to show it to Kenny when Randy had his celebration of life event for him. The event was still held as a celebration of his life and I showed everyone the film of Kenny.

Kenny's wife and parents were there. Randy and Kenny were very good friends. Ken really came from nowhere and rose to be a National Champion and he should have been on the Olympic Team. He was just a tough, tough guy. He was young when he died. He was only 50 or 51.

Chapter 8
Concord Cup

Bill Martel was on the National Coaching Staff for Greco-Roman for 25 years. To me he was hugely responsible for our success in the 1980s and 1990s at the World and Olympic Games in Greco because of the Concord Cup.

Olympic Team, 1988

When I got out of the military later on in the 1990s I went out to California and worked with him. He and I did that tournament through 1996.

Throughout the 1980s I took the Army Team to wrestle in the Concord Cup. Some of the greatest wrestlers from all over the world came and competed. We would take the winners and have a Gold Medal Match. They were the cream of the crop.

It took place in the ballroom of the Hilton in Concord. We would have special seating and lighting. We had raised mats like they did in the Olympics. There would be Opening Ceremonies and then the dual match.

We had a bar where you could sit and have cocktails while you were watching the match. The event was Bill Martel's baby. Each wrestler would get something for wrestling that night. One time we gave out gold watches that had Concord Cup on it. They were really nice watches that each athlete who wrestled would get.

We had Mikhail Mamiashili from Russia at one event. He was probably the best technician in the world at the time. He was a two-time Olympic Champion and numerous time World Champion.

Some countries, like Russia, did not come to train. They did not come for the competition. They had all the competition they needed in Europe and Russia.

They came to make money. We actually had to pay them to come over and wrestle. They came over and bought VCRs and things like that. They could not get that stuff in Eastern Bloc countries.

Mikhail was supposed to wrestle in the Gold Medal Match. It was going to be a big event with the local TV station there. At the last minute, Mikhail tried to back out. He claimed he had hurt his shoulder, which I knew was bullshit. He just did not want to wrestle.

We had marketed it and everyone was coming to see this Russian Champion and he was trying to be a no-show. I went and talked to him through an interpreter. I told him he was not going to receive his $500 gold watch if he did not wrestle. Of course, the watch was not worth that but he didn't know it. We bought in bulk and got them for $30 to $40 apiece. They were nice watches but not worth $500.

All of a sudden he says, "Oh, my shoulder feels better!" That night he wrestled, and of course, he pinned the American. He earned his gold watch.

We did that through the 1980s and we had dual matches all over California to promote the sport of Greco-Roman wrestling. Bill Martel did a lot and deserves the credit.

At Bill's house, he and his wife would host a social for all the coaches and referees. All the international coaches and referees would go to his house and they would have dinner catered and an open bar. It was a nice social event.

He got some money from USA Wrestling but it did not cover everything. So, we had to go out and beg, borrow, and steal to make these events happen. He had to get all the local high school coaches to load their mats up and bring them over in trucks. He would get sponsors from different businesses in the community to give money, and discounts from the hotel for the teams.

We were always trying to raise money for the Concord Cup. I also did private training during this time. One of the women I trained had a husband who worked for Bank of America. Through her it was set up that we would meet some people from the marketing department for Bank of America to see about getting sponsorship for the Concord Cup.

Bill bought a new suit so he would look good and presentable. We both went there thinking we would get $50,000 to $100,000 for the Concord Cup event. We had a video we showed and talked about the Olympics. After we left, we got a letter with a check in the mail. We were very excited to open it! We opened up the letter and there was a check for just $100. We were hoping for more but that is the way it went.

In 1985, I brought the Army Team out to the Concord Cup. My best friend Webbie was a fireman in L.A. at the time and he came to see me. He told me the L.A. Fire and Police Olympics were happening. They had boxing and he wanted me to coach him for a match.

He was going to fight an L.A. police officer. I told him I did not know anything about boxing. He said he would just feel better if I was there in his corner. I agreed to do it but I was crunched for time because my plane left at 11:00 PM and the boxing match was the same evening.

The fight was to take place at the Police Academy in L.A. When we were checking in for the fight, I had to ask them if Webbie could fight first so I could catch my plane. They agreed. They gave him a red uniform since he was an L.A. fire fighter and the police wore blue.

Webbie knew how to box. In college Webbie was a PAC 8 champion at Berkley. But he was close to forty years old and had not boxed in a while. The guy he was fighting was a cop in his twenties. That night the place was packed, they must have had 500 to 600 people there. They had ring girls there and everything.

Webbie and the police officer entered the ring and they made the announcement of L.A. Fire Dept. vs. L.A. Police Dept. Now, Webbie is not a mean individual. I gave him a pep talk about how he needs to protect himself, this guy could be dangerous. Before the fight, the coordinator called the police and fire departments together and told them, "Listen, you guys are professionals, nobody gets hurt.

Don't try to hurt anybody. Just go out there and give a good show because this is a fundraiser."

Webbie took this as gospel. He went out there and touched gloves with the cop and then went back to his corner. The bell rings and Webbie is jabbing and circling while the cop is throwing haymakers. He connects with one of them and Webbie drops like a sack of potatoes.

The referee began counting…5, 6, 7 and Webbie got to his feet with blood coming down into his mouth from his nose. Webbie held him off until the first round ended. I got a bag of ice and when he sat down, I put it on the back of his neck to try to shock him, wake him up a little bit.

I told him, "Webbie, this guy is trying to kill you, forget about being polite. Go out there and take care of him!" Webbie is in really good shape for being almost forty, he worked out every day running and lifting weights. The fight continued and the young police officer was getting really tired throwing all those haymakers. Halfway through the second period the police officer could not even hold his hands up. Webbie was connecting and he could have finished him off but he would not do it. I told him he should have knocked his ass out. At the end of the fight Webbie's hand was raised and he won the fight.

Webbie has a film of the fight. At the end of the first period the ring girls came out with signs, walking around the ring. It showed me looking at the ring girls. Webbie asked me, "Why were you looking at her and not me fighting?" I said, "Well, she's prettier than you!"

Anyway, after the fight he did not have time to change, just cut the hand wraps off so he could drive me to LAX. I was able to coach my best friend Webbie once, and he won! He did good. I was happy about that and felt relieved because his wife thought he might get brain damage or something from the fight, but it turned out just fine.

Getting back to wrestling, if the U.S. high schools wanted a clinic, they would have to put a request in to the commissions who were usually Olympic medalists, World Medalists, and coaches. The Hawaii High School Wrestling Association wanted a Greco and Freestyle clinic.

I was elected to lead the Greco Commission and two Olympic Freestyle Medalists were also elected to go. One was Russ Hellicason who was the coach of Ohio State for 20 years. He was also a silver medalist in the 1976 Olympics. Mark Schultz also went; he was a two-time World Champion and 1984 Olympic Gold Medalist in Los Angeles. Of course, I had been the Greco Assistant Olympic Coach.

I flew from New York, Russ from Ohio, and Mark from California to meet up in Hawaii. They picked us up and we went to what I believe was the Sheraton. It was right on the water and they had a beautiful golf course. We had a couple days before the clinics would start.

Russ brought his wife with him. Mark and I were by ourselves. At the hotel they put us in suites, Russ and his wife in one, Mark and I sharing another. Since we had a couple days, they asked us if we wanted to play some golf.

Russ was an avid golfer and had his own clubs, I did not play and neither did Mark. We all thought it would be a nice day to play and hit the ball around. We were down at the pro shop and they gave us golf clubs and a golf cart.

Then all of a sudden two big guys came up to us, they appeared to be Samoans. The manager of the hotel explained that these two big guys were going to go with us. I asked the manager, "Why are they going with us?" The manager replied, "They are for your protection. They are your security." I asked, "What do we need security for?" The manager explained that they had some people jump the fence and rob the golfers.

I told him, "You don't have to worry about us. I have two Olympic Champion wrestlers with me, and my 9-iron!"

The clinic was a three-day event and it went well. I was teaching Greco and they were teaching Freestyle. There were about 300 kids there over the three days.

There was a gentleman there from Korea by the name of Cho De Yun. In 1988 the Olympic Games were going to be in Seoul, Korea. He was on the Korean Olympic Committee for wrestling. He came to watch the clinic and to talk to us.

So, I met him and we hit it off because he is a retired Colonel in the Korean Army (ROK). He fought in Vietnam too, just like I had. He did not speak a word of English but he had an interpreter. We clicked right away because of Vietnam and wrestling.

He was a wealthy man. He owned an import/export business. He found out I was at the Military Academy at West Point and told me he had some business in New York. He asked if he could visit me at West Point next time he was in New York. I said, "Absolutely! Just call and let me know."

In 1986 Cho came to America. He was in New York and had a driver bring him to West Point. I met him at the gate to get him in. You have to have an ID to get in and I got him on base. I took him around and showed him West Point.

I had set it up with the Chief of Staff at West Point, a Colonel, that we would give him a West Point jacket as a gift. We had the Chief of Staff give him the jacket and show him around West Point. We took him to the wrestling room to have a look. Cho was very impressed and humbled by the attention he received. He left New York but we would soon meet again.

In 1986 I left West Point and was assigned to Fort Campbell, Kentucky. My friend Van Stokes was there. He was the Sports Director at Fort Campbell. We had been friends for many years. In the 1980s when I was going to Germany for the clinics for the Army, he was in some of the installations that set it up. They picked me up at the airport and worked with marketing. At night we would go out to a German restaurant and have a nice dinner and some German beer. We got to know each other and become friends because of this setup.

Van Stokes tells me that I am the reason he got involved with wrestling. Now, he is Vice President in charge of USA Wrestling for the United States. He has been on the board for about 20 years.

Van was heavily involved with the Board of Directors, he was a Treasurer, and has done a lot of leadership positions. He has also been Team Leader for World Championships, tournaments, and things like that.

Back at Fort Campbell, I had three more years until retirement. Van was there and he was the one who set up the lodging for the teams and dining facilities and so forth. He gave us an entire gym to train in for the wrestling team. It was a good partnership between him and I.

I had an office next to Van's in the Sports Office. While I was at Fort Campbell, Cho from Korea called again and came out to see me. At the base they have a museum for the 101st Airborne Division. It is quite a museum dedicated to the history of that division. I took Cho to the museum to see it.

In 1985, there was a horrible plane crash that killed 248 passengers and eight crew members headed back to their home base in Fort Campbell, KY. They were all members of the 101st Airborne Division. President Reagan came out to Fort Campbell after that to meet with the spouses and families who lost loved ones. In the museum they have pictures of Reagan hugging a wife and consoling family members. Cho was looking at it and he finally recognized what it was about.

He saw the President, the soldiers in the background, and the flag at half-mast and it clicked what it was about. Cho dropped to his knees, went into a prayer position, and started saying some prayers. He eventually got up and gave me a hug. I thought what he did showed great respect, after all, he was a soldier too.

I went and showed him around the base at Fort Campbell. We had another Colonel come in and gave him a 101st Airborne jacket. Once again, he was very impressed and honored by the attention he received.

In 1988, I flew out of San Francisco on a chartered flight for the Olympians to Seoul. Sitting right behind me was Flo-Jo, Florence Griffith Joyner, the Olympic Gold Medalist runner.

Jim Brown and Floyd Winter (left to right) in Seoul, South Korea, 1988

Our plane touched down in Seoul. We did not have to go through Customs, we just grabbed our bags and left the airport. I was the first one out of the airport and I was met by about 50 journalists with cameras and news crews. I said, "Wow! This is a lot of respect for a Greco-Roman coach." But they were waiting for Flo-Jo, not me.

I walked through them and there was Cho, waiting for me. We hugged each other and exchanged greetings. I told him through an interpreter that I had to get going because I had to take this bus to the Olympic Village. Cho said, "No, no, no! You are going to sleep at Cho's house!"

I told him, "I have to go to the Olympic Village." He responded, "I already talked to them and you are going with me." It is hard to say no to Cho. He had his driver take us to his house. He had this beautiful home overlooking the hills and Seoul. I walked in and saw rewards and medals, he had them all. He was a Brigade Commander in Vietnam.

We sat down and he went and got a bottle of Johnny Walker Red Scotch. Then he got some dried fish. We sat there and drank the scotch and ate the dried fish. He was showing me different things in his home. He had a picture of his mom and dad who were deceased, and explained he would say his prayers to them every night.

Bill Martel, Cho De Yun, and Floyd Winter (left to right) in Seoul, South Korea, 1988

He gave me some pajamas and I spent the night there. When I woke up in the morning my clothes had already been taken to a laundromat and dry cleaned. He drove me to the Olympic Village. Our team wrestled every day over the next several days. Every day he would have his driver waiting there to take me back to the Olympic Village so I would not have to take the bus. I remember the President of USA Wrestling coming out and he needed a ride. There was nobody there but Cho's chauffeur in a limousine picking me up. He said, "Floyd, I'm the President of USA Wrestling and you're just a coach and you have a limo driver and a chauffeur!" We gave him a ride and he was happy about it.

Cho would take me out at night and I got to meet his friends. You can have a suit for yourself made over there in one day. You go to the garment district, they measure you and everything, and it is done that night or the next morning. So, Cho took me down there to get a suit made. Honestly, I did not really want a suit but again, you can't say no to Cho.

So, I am there and the tailor is measuring how tall I am and my width and arm length and everything for my suit. I was supposed to get the suit the next day but the tailor said he could not do it for the next day. It would have to be the day after. Well, Cho did not like that and lit into him. He was chewing him out up and down and the guy was shaking. My suit was ready the next day.

Those were my dealings with Cho. He passed away years ago. I have nothing but fond memories of the man and the time we spent together. He was someone I met in my journey through life and I am glad that I did.

Chapter 9
Globe Trotting

I continued to do clinics all over America to promote the Army. We wanted to show people that the Army was more than just grenades and guns. I would send wrestlers or sometimes go myself. The parents, coaches, and kids would love it because they would get world class instruction at no cost to them. In return we would market the Army. So, it was a win-win situation.

I was the coach who went to Cuba to lead the Army Team in the Granma Cup. They invited several countries to go. Cuba is one of the best countries in the world for Greco.

Army Wrestlers receiving some awards after team workout (Photo Credit: Thomas, Tony)

We wrestled in a place called Las Tunas. You cannot get a direct flight from the U.S. to Havana. You have to go through Mexico or Caracas to catch a flight. I could not fly with the team because I was doing another clinic so I had to meet the team in Havana.

The same thing happened to me when I was selected to coach the U.S. Team in Hungary. I could not meet the team because I was busy doing something else. The team got there three hours before my plane landed in Budapest. My plane was late and I did not get there until midnight.

I arrived and there was nobody there to meet me. I found a police officer and made some calls. A little while later somebody came and got me and took me to their Olympic training facility and I was put up there. The next day they put me on a bus and told me I had to get off at some town and catch another bus.

I was really tired because I did not sleep that well the night before. It was really cold and I didn't have any blankets. So now I found myself on this crowded bus not knowing where I was going. I got a window seat and I knew I had two to three hours before I had to change buses, so I fell asleep.

While I was asleep this guy came and sat next to me with a pig in his hands. When I woke up that pig had his head on my chest and he was sleeping too! I eventually made it to the tournament for the weigh ins and wrestling.

Throughout the 1980s and 90s this is pretty much what I did. I traveled and coached different teams all over the world.

All Army Team, 1988 (Photo Credit: Thomas, Tony)

We had an international tournament in Rome. I ended up having lunch with the Mayor of Rome in his villa. It was catered outside and was really nice.

A few months later I coached a team at the World Championships in Norway. We had dinner at the castle where the King was. So, I was able to have lunch in Rome with the Mayor and dinner with the King in Norway at his castle.

I actually started researching my own ancestry and was able to go back about 500 years. My great-grandfather 14 times back was Sir William Winter. He was Queen Elizabeth the First's Admiral and a Knight. He fought in the armada against Spain back around 1580. His brother was Sir George Winter who was a Knight too. He actually still has a castle over in England.

I called the owners of the castle and they were pretty excited to hear from someone with an ancestry related to the castle. They said if I came over they would have some things for me and give me a tour. However, that is one place I have yet to visit.

In the early 1990s we had this facility at a fitness center in Walnut Creek, California. It was in the basement but it was nice, we had the mats down for our club. The owner sold the facility, though, and we had to leave. I had about 70 or 80 young kids in that club.

I found this empty building that was about the size of a two-car garage. We had one mat that went wall to wall. There was a bathroom there and I had a little office. It was kind of a dingy building but we were making the best of it.

We were in this league where we would wrestle other schools in junior high school. All the parents had to sit around the mats at our place because there was no seating. They would be screaming for their kids and the acoustics were pretty loud in there.

One night we had a whole bunch of matches and I noticed a gentleman standing there in hunting clothes. He had this hat on with the ear flaps down. I thought he was probably a grandfather of one of the kids. After the matches were over and everyone was leaving, he came up to me and asked if I was in charge.

I said, "Yes sir, I am." He said, "Well, I own this building." I responded, "I didn't know that." He went on to tell me that he loved what I was doing there for the kids. He said that he liked that the parents were involved and the kids were doing a physical activity and learning teamwork. He thought it was a beautiful thing.

He went on to say that boxing was important for him growing up. His name was Ken Hofmann. He was the owner of the Oakland Athletics and part owner of the Seattle Seahawks. He was a multi-millionaire. He said, "You need more room, don't you?" I said, "Well, we could use more room." He gave me his card and told me to call his business manager to set up a meeting with him.

I told Bill Martel and we went to a meeting a couple of days later. Ken was there with some other gentleman. We explained to him what we were doing with the kids and the wrestling club. Ken thought the kids being around Olympic coaches was wonderful. He knew we had no agenda; we were just there for the kids.

He asked me, "What do you need?" I said, "We could use more room or another mat." He said, "Okay, what else do you need?" I was hesitant to answer because I did not want to pile things on. He said, "Just tell me what you need. I think you need room for four mats. I am going to give you showers and weight equipment. Parents can't sit on the floor, so I'm going to give you bleachers."

I was thinking, "How is he going to do all of this?" The place we were in could only fit one mat. It turned out he owned the whole row of buildings next to the one we rented. He literally kicked everybody out and came in and remodeled everything.

He tore the walls down, set up the mats, and an office with a fax and phone. Bill and I were in awe that he would do all this! A boxing ring was put in there as well. It was like an MMA gym before MMA gyms were around.

It has been there ever since and it is still one of the better clubs in California.

In 1996, I left California and went back to West Point. I was offered a position as the Sports Director for the Child/Youth programs at West Point. I was able to stay involved with wrestling through the cadets on the West Point Team.

I applied for a job in Germany and I got it. I went over there as the Athletic Director in Bad Kreuznach, Germany. It was basically the same job I had at West Point but over in Germany.

I got involved with a German wrestling club in Mainz, Germany. I worked out there and trained the club. The Army Team came over in 2002 for the Armed Forces Championships and were going to wrestle in Russia so I set up a training camp for them.

In 2003 we hosted the High School European Championships in Germany. Usually, it would be held at some local gym but I wanted to upgrade the event. I talked to some of my friends in the German Federation and we got this beautiful Sports Hall to host them. It was similar to a World Olympics event.

The General came to the event and a couple of Germans who were World Olympic medalists. They did a clinic for the kids. Everyone really enjoyed it and it turned out to be a nice event.

I headed back to West Point after this. I came back once again as the Sports Director for the youth programs. I liked West Point and also coaching and training in Germany. These two places played a critical role in my life and I went back and forth between the two of them.

In 2005 in Concord, California, I was selected to be the coach for the World Cup U.S. Team. The World Cup is the best team from each continent. They would wrestle to find out who has the best team. The competition was in Lund, Sweden.

We trained in Gothenburg, Sweden. I took the USA Team there and we trained there for about eight days. Then we went down to Denmark. The Soviets were there, Cuba, Bulgaria, Japan, Sweden, and others.

We wanted to invite the Russians back to America for the Concord Cup. They were the best in the world at Greco. They are a big draw too because they have numerous Olympic Champions on their team. I think they had four or five that year.

The Russians' coach was an Olympic Champion. They wanted me to talk to him and invite his team to compete back at the Concord Cup in America. He did not speak English, but told me through an interpreter that after the tournament we would talk.

At a banquet after the tournament, he came and sat down at my table. He brought his interpreter and two bottles of vodka. We got a couple of tall glasses and he filled both of them to the top with vodka. He chugged his down and then looked at me. I am thinking, "What the hell…" He was a small guy too. I told myself, "I am not going to let this Russian outdo me." So, I chugged mine down too. I was 48 years old at the time.

We started talking. With the Russians it was always more of a financial thing. I did not have the final say in anything but kept playing along. He kept pouring tall glasses full of vodka. Over the next 45 minutes I had about five tall glasses of vodka. I was a hurtin' weasel.

In the morning I had to catch a train and then a boat. I lay down in my room for about an hour and then I threw up. I had to get up to catch the train though. Then I took a hydrofoil that took about an hour. I was sick as hell, turning purple, green, and any color in between. The wrestlers said, "Coach, you don't look well." I just said, "I'm okay."

I did get an agreement with the Russians to come and what the finances would be. They did show up next year and it was good. Actually, Randy Couture got to wrestle one of the best wrestlers in the world because of it.

In 2007 I went to Antalya, Turkey, for the world Sambo Championships. It was interesting because we did "beach wrestling" while we were there. Oil wrestling is their sport in Turkey. They wear leather pants and put olive oil all over their bodies. You are like a greased pig. It was a very interesting experience.

Chapter 10

Golden Years

After West Point, I applied for three other jobs, one in Germany, one in Italy, and one at Joint Base McGuire in New Jersey. I ended up getting all three jobs. My wife wanted to go to Italy of course, because she is Italian. Our daughter was living in New Jersey, though, so we chose Joint Base McGuire.

I worked for the Department of Defense as an Athletic Director. I spent the next 11 or 12 years in New Jersey. I was still heavily involved with wrestling. I traveled and coached numerous World Teams and officiated Varsity Wrestling.

I had the opportunity to be in good places throughout the years. I spent nine years at West Point. I was a part of that institution where they make leaders. It greatly impacted me.

If I did not come back to be a Sports Director it would be a dull time for me. I would not really have anything to do. I could not just go to work for eight hours and then go home. I am not that type and enjoyed using my experience to be able to help the military and civilian communities.

Floyd Winter (third from left)

I also ran the sports and fitness programs for the installation. That entails overseeing fitness instructors, aerobics instructors, fitness/weight machines, and the general facility. We ran intramural programs such as basketball and soccer.

I did other things there too that I am proud of. We had this large field at Fort Dix. It was not really being used for anything at the time. I thought we should be using this and making some money. So, I talked to the New Jersey Soccer Organization. They said that they wanted to put on tournaments. It was so large we could put 20 soccer fields there.

Usually, you cannot find a place that large. I finally got everything approved. There were obstacles because the base was secure. You could not get on the base unless you were military or had a pass. I was able to work around that. They would send the names from the teams and I worked with them.

I did the marketing. We actually made about $12,000 to $15,000 a weekend. The soccer teams paid for the fields. For the seven years I was there, we made almost $500,000 from it.

Because of that I was able to get a million-dollar renovation done to Griffiths Field House at Fort Dix. I put in the justification and all the paperwork. I sent it in and it was approved. They put in new floors, equipment, showers, and locker rooms. I felt good about that.

I also had the Philadelphia Eagles cheerleaders come to the gym. They put on a cheerleading show. It was a successful event that was done for the military. They did not even charge us for coming out because they did it for our military.

Those are some of the events I did besides wrestling.

I also set up a boxing match between the Golden Gloves of New Jersey and the Marine Corps boxing team from Camp Lejeune at Joint Base McGuire. I had to get the officials, set up a boxing ring, and market it. I got "Smokin'" Joe Frazier to come and be the honored guest and hand out the medals.

Floyd Winter, Wayne Wells, and Vince Zurao (left to right)

The whole place was packed to get Joe's autograph. He actually helped coach some of the Marines. When I was in Fort Bragg in 1972 the Army had their boxing team there and guess who came to see them? Smokin' Joe Frazier! If you have a facility and the backing of command you can do things like that.

In October of 2014 Randy Couture came out for the World Military Championships that I hosted at the Air Force Base in New Jersey. We had 24 countries attend the Championships. I had the awards banquet as the finale on the Battleship Missouri across from Philadelphia. That is where I received an award and was Knighted by the International Military Sports Council (CISM). It was a great honor that I did not expect.

Floyd Winter being Knighted by the International Military Sports Council

Medal pinned on Floyd Winter at the Knight Ceremony

We had the event catered and all the participants really enjoyed it. I called in a favor from West Point and they sent their band down. I also called the Philadelphia Eagles and got their cheerleaders to come.

It was a huge event. We sort of shut the whole base down. We did not charge for the event. It was open to the community. They had a chance to come and see all these Olympic and World medalists. We had over 20 Olympic and World medalists wrestle and thirty women who wrestled. We had over 220 wrestlers from all over the world and had to organize the transportation, lodging, and dining facilities for them.

We had an autograph session for Randy Couture and the Eagles Cheerleaders. Randy had a booth and the cheerleaders had another one. All the wrestlers knew Randy because he was a multiple time UFC Champion, so we figured his booth would be packed. We were wrong, everyone lined up to get the Philadelphia Eagles Cheerleaders autographs!

As far as Greco-Roman Wrestling is concerned, it does not always get the love that Freestyle does. One of the most feared wrestlers in history was a Greco-Roman wrestler by the name of Aleksandr Karelin. His nickname was "The Russian Bear." He had 420 wins and only one loss. He won three Olympic Gold Medals and a silver.

Greco-Roman wrestling is just different. For instance, they have thinner mats in high school. The international mats are much thicker. In international you can lift your opponent off the mat and throw, you can do belly to backs. That is illegal in high school because of injuries to the neck and shoulder areas. Since it is illegal in high school, they do not learn the correct technique.

Later on, when they wrestle internationally, that is when they learn the skills. By then, you have to compete against guys from Europe and Asia who have been wrestling their whole lives. In some countries Greco-Roman is their number one sport.

The military now has the best Greco-Roman program in the United States. The wrestlers in the military are the best athletes in the military. Greco-Roman wrestling is one of the best systems for hand-to-hand combat. A Greco-Roman wrestler can do a lot of damage to someone.

Take Randy Couture, for example. He was a five-time MMA World Champion. I remember him at Fort Campbell,

Kentucky, when they had jump school. Part of it was combatives. They had this pit with sawdust. The soldiers had to go in there while someone else tries to throw them out. One of the commanders asked if I would bring Randy over.

He was the Armed Forces Champion at the time. They asked if I could bring him over to see if they could throw him out of the pit. I said, "Sure." Randy threw about ten of them out of the pit like rag dolls without even breaking a sweat.

Nevertheless, I believe there are numerous things you need to possess to be a successful athlete and wrestler. To be a Champion. The number one thing is that you have to earn it. If you have not earned it you are not entitled to it. It is not by chance, or magic, or lady luck. How do you earn it? You earn it by making the extra effort. The extra effort is you do not miss practice, you stay after practice and drill, and you never miss a weight date.

I also do not see how you expect to win if you are not in better shape than everyone you wrestle.

Many times, when you wrestle, you are sick and hurt when competing. Especially in the finals, you do not go through a tough tournament without some sort of injury. It takes a lot to overcome these injuries and step on the mat. Even if you are losing by points in the final minute, you have to believe that you are going to come back and win. I have seen many athletes overcome injuries and win. They would not quit.

Another quality a Champion possesses is that you have to believe in yourself. You have to believe in yourself when no one else does. You have to believe in yourself when you are sick and hurt. You have to believe that you are going to win. The ones who win the medals are the ones who believe in themselves.

Those are some of the key lessons I think you need to succeed, not only in wrestling, but in life as well.

I have reached my 70s and I cherish my time with family and friends. I also still love to travel. I have kept busy being a guest speaker at more than 300 different events.

My best friend Webbie and I still see each other several times a year. When I visit him, he picks me up at the San Francisco Airport. We have friends all over California. We head south, down toward Monterey. We crisscross the state of California visiting friends and family. We cut over to Porterville where we were both born and raised. We laugh as we are driving down 101 or 99 in California…just two old guys having fun and philosophizing about life.

Floyd Winter (left) with Webbie at Floyd's son's wedding in Philadelphia, 2010

About twelve years ago, Paula applied for her flight attendant job to be stationed out of Frankfurt, Germany. Her airline commutes to numerous cities back in the United States from there. She has had an apartment in Germany ever since. I have been able to fly with her numerous times over the years and we stay together at the apartment in Frankfurt. It really has been a wonderful experience. She now has 25 years in as a flight attendant.

Last year we flew with our grandson to Prague, Turkey, and Denmark. She gets to fly for free and as her spouse I get that benefit too. We plan on doing a lot more traveling in the future.

Now we live in Maryland. Paula flies in and out of Dulles International Airport in Virginia. Her company puts her up in a nice hotel if she cannot make it home in time for her next shift. I go down and meet her at the hotel and we have dinner and I spend the night with her. The next day she goes back to the airport and I come home. Sometimes I bring one of the grandkids with me to stay at the hotel and swim. They love it.

Without Paula in my corner as my wife and my biggest supporter, I could not have accomplished everything I did. Being a military spouse is difficult because their husband is often gone. She was left at home by herself with the kids. When the kids were sick, something broke, or the bills needed to be paid, she was there by herself. My war days were over but I still did a lot of traveling with my wrestling and coaching career. She was my inspiration and held everything together.

With me coaching and wrestling all over the world and her flying everywhere for work, we had a pretty international lifestyle.

In the Army we were soldiers. The ones who earned their way onto the All Army Team were held in high esteem. You had to survive the training. You had to earn it. Nobody gave you anything.

I decided to write this book because of the friendships I developed over the years through wrestling.

It did not matter to me if you were an Olympic Champion or not. We were a team and you were a part of it. I believed in you. The most important thing was making that *great effort*.

Everybody cannot win. Winning is important, but if you can beat yourself and be a better person, leader, or commander for it, that means everything. This is especially true in the Army where you have to lead men into combat.

Every day, get up, put your shoes on, and do the best you can. That is all I cared about, not the color of the medal. Just do the best you can. Every day do your best to improve. Normally, if you do that, great things will happen.

I had to be their father, mother, priest, and shoulder to cry on. I had to yell at them and hold them. Everyone was unique. I loved them all.

Stay Low and Circle Left.

~ Floyd Winter

Afterword
Lives Touched by
Floyd "Bad News" Winter

Floyd Winter

When I was approached to write this book, I had no idea the impact it would have on my own life. I met Floyd at a catch wrestling seminar several years ago. He was probably in his late sixties at the time, and the man was a legend.

However, I really did not know much about him. I remember him methodically coaching me on the details of how to do a single leg takedown on my opponent. I had no idea at the time that I would be writing a book in the future about this man's extraordinary life journey. It would be several years before I spoke to or saw Floyd "Bad News" Winter again.

Floyd Winter (left) and author Daniel DiMarzio

Fast forward several years and I am starting to write a book about my coach, Joel Bane. He called me one day and said, "I want you to put our book on hold. There is someone who deserves it more than me. His name is Floyd "Bad News" Winter and he has one hell of a story to tell." A meeting was set up between Floyd, Joel, and me.

The rest is history.

I spent countless hours interviewing Floyd. It was immediately apparent this man had a unique story to tell. He is an American hero and I wanted to get his story down on paper for future generations. Many of the stories written in this book have never been told before.

I went to his home and met his beautiful wife and family. We spent the day together and it was obvious the love he had for his wife, children, and grandchildren. While I was there his wife, Paula, spirited me off to another room. She said, "Here is a note Floyd left for me this morning. I want people to know just how sweet Floyd really is."

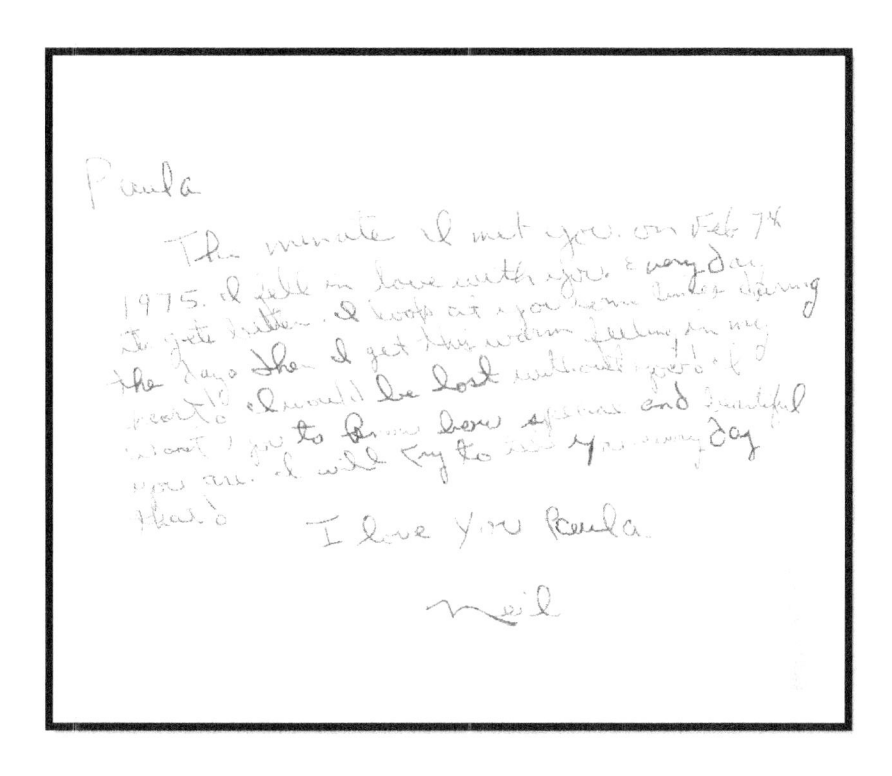

A letter from Floyd to his wife Paula

Floyd made it clear he did not want this book to be just about him. He formed close bonds with many of the people he met along the way during his incredible journey. He told me, "These people deserve this book more than I do. I learned from them and they learned from me. They made me who I am today. It was about friendship and camaraderie."

I was soon given a list of people for me to contact and interview. It was impressive. The names included generals, colonels, special forces operatives, Olympic medalists, movie stars, and civilian success stories. Floyd told me, "Talking to these people will change your life."

He was right. They were extraordinary individuals with distinguished careers, each with their own story. The stories these individuals would tell about Floyd could fill a whole other book. They all credited Floyd "Bad News" Winter with helping them reach their goals and positions in life.

Simply saying Floyd's name would cause them to open up to me like a friend whom they had known for years. Floyd's name opened doors that would have otherwise remained shut. The depth of knowledge I gleaned from these individuals about life, camaraderie, and service to one's country was boundless.

Floyd stated, "The whole time it was about making great efforts, and even when you came up short it did not affect your friendships. Many of them did come up short, but they became better for it. They became better leaders and better people because of it."

Speaking with Floyd for hours on end as the days and months ticked by had its own impact on me. His lifetime of great experience, adventure, and accomplishment inspired me. I could not help but think many Americans would feel the same way, especially in these troubling and uncertain times.

Floyd Winter is a rare breed, a truly unique person. One who not only is gifted physically through hard work and sacrifice, but socially as well, able to reach the common man and upper echelons of society alike with his charismatic wit and charm.

Floyd "Bad News" Winter has touched countless lives. The following are some of their stories…

~ Daniel DiMarzio
Philadelphia, Pennsylvania
December 2020

I did not even know they had an All Army Wrestling team when I enlisted. I was in the 2nd Ranger Battalion. The Battalion participated in three sports at Fort Lewis: cross country, wrestling, and boxing. They usually won every one of those.

We were deployed and we had a party. I do not remember where we were, but there was a guy there who could literally pick up the front end of a jeep. We were wrestling and I beat his ass. The commander came out and said, "You are going to go and try out for Battalion Wrestling."

I had wrestled in high school and one year in college. Then I joined the Army. I got on the team and there was a guy who I wrestled and beat who was on the All Army Wrestling Team. So, I asked him, "How do you get on the All Army Team?" He told me you have to apply and be selected.

So, I applied and I never got accepted. I knew a guy named Captain Jackman who knew Floyd. He was from West Point and that is where Floyd was stationed at the time. He called Floyd up and talked to him and Floyd said he would give me a chance.

I went and tried out for the All Army Wrestling Team. I went there and there were nine people in my weight class. I had to wrestle every one of them twice. I lost one match. I had to wrestle one of them again because I was kind of a nobody, I had not done anything. I ended up making the team.

I made the team because Floyd gave me the opportunity. Floyd was an exceptionally good coach. I had never wrestled Greco-Roman in my life. He literally took me from scratch and taught me everything I knew.

He was also good enough to bring talent in. He would bring people to show us their best move. You learned a lot just from Floyd but you also learned a lot from the other people. If Floyd had not been a wrestling coach, he should have been a track coach. We ran our asses off. The camp was at Fort Bliss and we would run to the gate. I do not know how far that was, five or six miles or something. I was a relatively good runner. That was on the days that we would lift weights.

The days we did not lift weights we ran sprints. Depending on what kind of mood ol' Floyd was in was how many sprints we would run. They were 220s and 440s because it was an old track. Half the team would be on one side and the other half on the other side and you would run sprints. I just remember that whistle never stopped blowing.

We had two to three practices a day. You had sprinting/running in the morning and weightlifting. Then you had technique practice where Floyd taught us technique. Then in the evening you had scrimmage practice where you applied what you learned that day. In the two or three months that we had the camp prior to going to the Interservice tryouts, I went from not knowing how to wrestle Greco, to that first year placing fifth in the Nationals. That is from never having done it in my life.

He is the best coach I ever had. I had some really good coaches, too. I had a guy named Greg Nelson who coached me in high school. He was an All American and he taught me a lot. He taught me how to do a cradle. The first year I went to college I wrestled for a guy named Mike Clock. He was a good coach, too. When I got out of the Army and went to college, I did not have a good coach though. A good coach makes a difference.

We went to the Interservice and I did not win it but ended up second. However, the guy who was supposed to go to the CISMs could not go so I went. We went to Venezuela for that.

The thing I always remember about Venezuela is that the Iranians were wrestling in the CISMs. One of the Iranians came up to me and said, "Hey, I want to defect." I did not know what to do, so I went to Floyd. Floyd got hold of somebody from the Embassy. We were all staying in the barracks and literally in the middle of the night you could see these bags getting thrown out of a window. All of these Iranians ran out and jumped into a van. I do not know what Floyd did, or who he talked to, but all those guys defected. Remember, this was during the Iraq/Iran war and they were slaughtering each other.

The wrestling was done and we went to the Marine barracks for a party. Floyd was drinking beer. The whole time I knew Floyd he would always be standing on his hands and walking around. He could walk on his hands better than I could walk on my feet. Floyd had a long neck beer bottle in his mouth. He walked down the Marine barracks stairs on his hands with that beer bottle in his mouth the whole way. He was drinking it as he was walking down the damn steps! It was just unbelievable.

That summer we got called back for the World Team tryouts. We were training for the CISMs and then we came back and tried out for the World Team. When we were at the tryouts there Floyd would tell us stories about Vietnam.

We were sitting in the dayroom when he told us these stories. He told me he was out there in the jungle and they had dogs to help them out. He said, "All we ever got were damn C-rations and the dog always got steak!" He told me a story of how he was trying to steal the steak away from the dog with a stick and the dog came after him. He was out there in the middle of Vietnam trying to steal that dog's chow!

The next year after wrestling the Interservice at Quantico we went up to wrestle in Sambo. I had never even heard of Sambo. It was held at some place near Washington, D.C. Our first year we actually placed really high in Sambo even though we had never wrestled in it before. Next year our team did even better in it. If I am not mistaken, I think we won the Nationals that year. Floyd had never wrestled in it or coached it and in two years he was dominating Sambo. It was because he was just such a good coach.

I won the CISMs twice, two years in a row in Freestyle.

The next time I got associated with the All Army Team I was in the 3rd Ranger Battalion at Fort Benning. I would go practice with them because they were stationed at Fort Benning. Tony Thomas was the coach at that point. Floyd had retired.

The toughest guy I ever wrestled was Steve Fraser. Not only did he beat you in the score, he physically beat you like you came out of a boxing match.

During my time wrestling for the All Army Team, I got to wrestle many high-level wrestlers. I wrestled with eight Olympic or World Champions. That is where I came up with this expression that there is a difference between *confidence* and *conceit*.

Every single one of those guys during tryouts would show you their best move. They would drill and drill you on that move until you could do it well. Then you would go and wrestle off with them. It did not matter that they had showed you their best move because they knew they were going to win. They never once would say a word about themselves. That is the difference between *confidence* and *conceit.*

Floyd was a really good coach and I have nothing to say but good things about the man. I have kept in touch with Floyd Winter my whole life.

~ Chris Pease

I first saw Coach Winter in 1979 or 1980 when I went up to a wrestling tournament in New York. It was a regional Greco tournament. I was still wrestling in college at the time. There was some banter going around about how "Bad News" is wrestling! "Bad News" is coming out of retirement! He's wrestling!" I was like, "What the hell are they talking about?"

At the time I had no idea who Floyd "Bad News" Winter was. I got to see him wrestle and he destroyed the competition in the tournament. I found out that he had already retired and came back just to have some fun, I guess.

At the time I was wrestling in college and I had heard of the Army Team and the Marine Team. They were at the tournament. I realized how incredible these guys were and what level they were at. I wrestled a Marine guy and he threw me around like a rag doll.

A couple years later after college, I joined the Army. I got stationed over in Europe. I really wanted to join the All Army Wrestling Team because I knew they were phenomenal athletes who competed at all levels. In order to make the Army Team back then you had to go through a successive number of tournaments. You had to take a gold medal in both Freestyle and Greco.

Floyd Winter, the Army Coach, would fly over to watch the tournament to see what guys he wanted to bring back. I was sitting in the gym getting ready for the tournament when I heard people saying, "Floyd Winter's here! Floyd, Floyd Winter's here!" It was almost like this mystical god was sitting in the stands. Everybody was looking at him and people were trying to come up and see him.

I still did not know him at all. I won some gold medals and was fortunate enough to be selected to go back. I remember him walking up to me. I am a thin guy by nature. I wrestled at 180 pounds but I really weighed 194 or 195 pounds at the time. Floyd said, "You did a good job. We'll see you at 163 pounds." I was thinking to myself, "What!?" But, I said "Yeah coach, 163!" I thought, "There is no way…" That was my first meeting with him face-to-face, it only lasted about 20 seconds.

I walk into camp and I am seeing all these national level place winners and guys who were on the World Team. I was in awe the first time I went and tried out for the Army Team.

I remember Floyd coming in that first practice when we were at Fort Devens. He just made everybody kind of calm down. His personality is such that it is kind of low key and he had a nice calming effect, especially for the new rookies coming in. He made you feel at ease, but you also felt uptight. You wanted to make the team and you were in the presence of a wrestling legend. Floyd was the first American to ever win a World Title in Greco-Roman wrestling. He was the all-time Armed Forces Gold Medalist, former National Champion, and all these things.

Quickly we realized what Floyd really brought. He was able to be a coach, mentor, and at the same time a good friend. He treated us like adults unlike in high school or college where the coaches were more like, "You do as I say and as I do." Floyd still had the ability to do that but might say after practice, "Let's go out for a beer!" So, you had this adult to adult relationship.

This was a unique style of coaching. On other teams I had been on as an adult no one else did that. You had your coach and there was a wall. Kind of like in the military between supervisors and subordinates. Floyd was able to break that wall down with his wrestlers. As a coach he knew the bigger picture. He was not just a coach. He had influence, and was able to gain influence, at the highest levels of the Department of the Army and Department of Defense. He was able to build and create what would be considered the start of the greatness of the Army Teams. He built those foundations.

People like General Moore and Chief of Staffs would come in and they would talk to Floyd, as Floyd, not Sergeant Winter. It was unique he was able to do that and bring down their guards. After a couple years on the team he brought me around a little bit to see and work with him on some of these things. People just really opened their doors and admired Floyd as an administrator, a thinker, and a developer of an organization with goals and values. It was an extraordinary sight to see. He had a natural gift to get people on his camp, on his side.

We had a guy on our team who was a 198 pounder who had just finished second in the nation. He wanted to get out of the Army. He told Floyd, "Hey, I'm getting out." Floyd asked, "Why?" and the guy said, "I don't like what I'm doing in the Army etc." He had a skillset for a position that no longer existed in the Army that he wanted to do. Floyd was able to pull strings and get him that position even though it no longer existed in the Army.

I myself was thinking of getting out of the Army. I actually put my packet to get out of the Army. It was offseason and Floyd called me out of the blue. He said, "Hey, Chuck, I got your invitation. You are going to the National Camp." I said, "Oh Coach, I think I might be getting out of the Army." He replied, "Why are you getting out of the Army? You could still go but it would be on your own dime." I said, "If I stayed in the Army, Coach, could I still go?" He said, "Absolutely!"

I went down to see my boss. I said, "Hey, I want to stay in the Army!" He said, "Huh!?" They were able to get my orders pulled. My branch manager who was a Lieutenant Colonel said, "What's going on here? You were getting out now you're going to this wrestling thing?" She was going to assign me to this obscure position so I could not go to the National Camp.

I called Coach and said, "Listen, I can't go." He said, "Hang on!" I responded, "Okay…" The next day I got a call from my branch manager, she was really pissed off. She said, "Who the hell…you got the Chief of Staff on me! All right, you go where you want. Where do you want to be assigned?" I was like, "Huh?" Floyd had gone all the way up to the Chief of Staff of the Army so that I could get my orders changed so I could get assigned where I wanted. I could not believe it.

Like I said, he was more than just a coach to the Army athletes. He really understood how to work the system and people really liked him. He was not a fiery guy. He was even keeled and nothing seemed to rile him.

One time the team was training hard, beating each other up, and cutting weight. A big fight broke out. Floyd had stepped away and was not there. He came back in and punches were flying. He walked in and with just his *presence*, everybody stopped. There were five or six guys going at it and he just walked in and did not say anything. He did not have to break it up, everyone just stopped fighting. Then he blew his whistle and said, "All right, let's get back to practice."

We had a guy who was a 149 pounder ranked top two or three in the nation. His unit was with the 82nd Airborne Division. He was a top-notch soldier. He loved soldiering as much as he loved wrestling. He was a squad leader. He came up to Army camp and received a notification that the members of his squad were all killed in a helicopter accident.

He was devastated. He went to the Officer's Club when he was an NCO. He was not supposed to do that, you just do not go there. He started drinking. All his buddies, all his comrades, the people he was responsible for were dead. Now, he feels guilty because he was not there.

Somebody asked him, "Who are you? What are you doing here?" The next thing you know he had hit somebody at the club. Now, he is getting hauled away. In a normal situation that soldier, our guy, would have been court martialed.

Floyd went to bat for him. He went in there and explained the situation to the Commanding General of the Base. He was able to get everything resolved and nobody got in trouble. Let's face it, everyone knew the soldier was sad, but he wasn't supposed to go where he went and wasn't supposed to be drinking. Somebody challenged him and he hit them. Floyd was able to smooth all that over without any issues.

The other thing that made Floyd unique was, I do not know much about his upbringing, but there had to be a little street hustler in him. He was not just a good pool player…he could hustle *anybody*. We were out once with our teammates and somebody challenged us to a bet. Floyd bet the guy he could beat him at pool and use a broomstick instead of a pool cue.

It was hilarious, the guy left furious because Floyd took him to the cleaners! He would meet people at the bar and they did not know he wrestled or anything. He did not have that quote-unquote "Wrestlers physique." He was tall and lanky and looked like a ping pong player. It was offseason and we were all sitting around the bar. Floyd started talking to some guys whom he did not know.

The guys were trying to brag about what they could do. Floyd was like, "Well, I can walk on my hands blah, blah, blah." He was tipsy. He then said, "Yeah, I can walk up those stairs on my hands." These people did not believe him. Floyd said, "I'll bet you a $100!" Everybody cleared out and hundreds of dollars were thrown down because these people did not know who he was. He was inebriated but walked on his hands all the way up the flight of steps and all the way back down. He took all their money! It was amazing how he was able to maneuver these people into a little bit of a hustle.

We were younger than he was, he was a decade or a decade and a half older than us, doing these things that we could not even do.

He was also strict about what he said. He would give everyone a strike or two. I will give you one of my personal examples. We were at the Olympic Training Center and I met this girl. We were flying back soon and I asked her to go out to dinner. I figured I would go out to dinner and come back and pack. Well, it proceeded past there. I called Randy and told him I am going to miss the flight tomorrow. Tell Coach something came up. About three days later I got a flight back to practice.

I came walking in like, "Uh-oh." He looks at me and says, "Sounds like you had a good time." I said, "Yeah, Coach." He said, "I hope it was worth it." I am like, "Uhhh…yeah it was." He goes, "Okay, now we are going to go do an hour and a half worth of sprints."

He stood there and just *tortured* me. I was 99% of the time the good guy on the team. We had some guys who had personalities that were, you know…would pull some antics. Floyd would give you that little bit, but I knew I could never do anything again. I paid for my sin. He said, "Now you've done your penance, go back and start practicing."

After two consecutive years in a row I was injured. I blew out one knee and the next year I blew out the other. That normally would have been it, but Coach came to me and said, "You definitely aren't the most talented guy on this team Chuck, but you've got more heart and work hard. You're gonna come back and we are going to give you the opportunity to make the team again."

Normally, any other coach would have said you are done, you are out of here. But Floyd really looked at people and saw what they were made of. It was not necessarily because of talent that he would keep somebody on the team. The other thing was that he could spot talent like nobody else's business.

Randy Couture was an eighteen-year-old kid just out of high school when most of the guys on the team had at least some type of college background. Floyd just saw in this young guy that he could be a world level athlete. Floyd would see guys at tournaments and everybody else would be like, "Eh, nothing special." Floyd would say, "I want that guy, that guy's got something there." He could convince people to come into the Army to wrestle because of his personality. He had the ability to look at talent that should be on the team and was able to get them.

Randy was one of those classic guys whom Floyd saw talent in. When he first saw him, Randy had a very tough weight class. You usually only keep two guys per weight class, that is the Army rules. Floyd said nope, I am going to keep a third guy and that guy is Randy. So, he brought him back to train. Randy has never looked back since. From then on Randy's career skyrocketed.

As Floyd and I got older we developed a really good, friendly relationship. He and his wife Paula are like family to me. He would bring you into his house if you needed something. He was always there. He has always been giving to everybody.

He had a great way of getting the best out of his athletes to meet their potential. He took a guy like Derrick Waldroup who had great potential, but I do not think realized it, and Floyd molded him. Derrick said, "I don't want to wrestle that Greco crap. I'm a Freestyler!" Floyd told him, "No, you're not a Freestyler. You're a Greco guy." Derrick said, "No coach, I ain't wrestling that crap!" After a number of weeks of Floyd working with him in Greco, he went and won the Armed Forces Championships. His rookie year he won the National Championship. He did not even have any losses. He then went on to be an Olympian.

I have had tons of coaches but Floyd is just a unique personality all the way across the board. You have the compassionate guy, the intellectual guy, the hard-ass coach guy, and then you have the street hustler guy. All those traits are wrapped into one person with Floyd Winter.

~ Chuck Africano

I met Floyd Winter in 1982 while he was conducting a wrestling clinic for the U.S. Army soldiers in Europe. At the time I was a soldier wrestling for Wildflecken, Germany. It was very impressive to see him lead the practice himself. He showed us cross training techniques by doing them himself first: flips, walking down the mats on his hands etc.

In 1983 Floyd Winter invited me to attend the All Army Wrestling camp in Fort Bliss, Texas to try out for the All Army Wrestling Team. There were two things that I lacked in 1983, confidence and discipline. Floyd Winter was instrumental in developing both.

In 1983 at Fort Bliss, the Bell twins, Donnell and Arnell Bell, Phil Godbolt and I decided to walk to practice. We arrived late and everyone was already putting on their wrestling shoes. The four of us put our shoes on and we started to practice. Floyd conducted practice and never said anything about us arriving late. As soon as practice was over Coach Winter said, "I need to see the twins, Tony Thomas and Phil Godbolt."

He told us, "You guys were late to practice. You have an excellent chance to train with the best wrestler in the USA. You cannot waste this opportunity." He then took us to the athletic track and made us run sprints: 100 meters, 200 meters and 400 meters over and over again. It felt like an hour. I wanted to quit so bad. After that day I no longer had a discipline problem. From that day on I made sure I was very early to practice. If I was not the first one there I made sure to be there at least thirty minutes early.

Somehow, Floyd saw something in me that I could not see in myself. Floyd would often introduce me to other coaches on the USA National Greco-Roman Coaching staff. He would say, "This is Tony and he is going to be a National

Champion." I remember one coach smiled and asked Floyd, "In what?" Floyd said, "In Greco-Roman Wrestling."

In 1984 I was at the Final Olympic Trials in Allendale, MI after winning the mini tournament. They were at Grand Valley College. I was wrestling John Guira in the best two out of three matches. In the second match, I was attempting a head lock and was stopped in the middle of the throw. I was then driven headfirst into the mat. That is all I can remember. Somehow, I could hear them saying that I was not breathing and had no pulse. I was trying to answer, "I can hear you." When I came to, I was strapped to a stretcher and on my way to the hospital.

I was visited in the hospital by Romey Pelletier, my Army teammate. He explained to me what had happened. Romey informed me that I was unconscious with no pulse and had swallowed my tongue. He told me that Floyd Winter performed CPR and saved my life.

All I know is that when I was revived, I asked them to let me up because I was a medic, and there was nothing wrong with me. I must have been in bad shape because my Army job was a Calvary Scout, not an Army Medic.

When Floyd Winter came to the hospital he told me to call my mother. The story was on television and in the USA Today newspaper. After being released from the hospital, Floyd arranged for me to travel to Walter Reed Army Hospital in Washington, DC to be checked out. The next year he arranged for me to attend a sports clinic at the Olympic Training Center, in Colorado Springs, CO where athletes were taught how to properly maintain a healthy diet. He sent me because he believed the cause of my injury was the way I cut weight to make 149.5 pounds.

I continued to wrestle from 1984 through 1988. During those four years Floyd had more confidence in my ability than I did myself. He would often tell me there is no one in the 149.5 pounds or 163 pounds weight class better than you. He would tell us stories after practice about the three combative sports in the Ancient Olympic Games. After these stories we were motivated to practice even harder.

Floyd Winter spent countless hours attempting to build my wrestling confidence. He would bring wrestlers in to train with from other teams. They had teammates in my weight class and after practice he would ask the other wrestlers, "Who is better Tony or your teammate?"

Floyd Winter's practices were extremely difficult. We would start practice in the morning with running. Monday, Wednesday, and Friday we would run sprints at the track. We would run 100-meter, 200-meter and 400-meter sprints. Some days we would run up to five miles of sprints in combinations of 20 to 40 100-meter sprints, four to eight 200-meter sprints, then two 400-meter sprints.

I can still hear Floyd Winter saying, "Sprint Tony. It's not a jog, it's not a run, it's a sprint!" Sometimes we would run 10 to 20 200-meter and four 400-meter sprints. On the days we did not do sprints we would do five-mile runs. When we started and ended we had to endure Floyd saying, "IT'S NOT A JOG! IT'S NOT A RUN! IT IS A FIVE MILE SPRINT!!!" I can still feel that wind hitting my face and driving me back as we ran from the gym to the Fort Bliss, TX Base gate, and back, in 1983.

After running we would go directly to morning mat practice. Floyd's practices were cross-training before cross-training was even heard of. We would start practice with gymnastics warm-ups: cartwheels, diving forward rolls, front handsprings, front handsprings off another wrestler's back, and front handsprings over two or three wrestlers side by side. Then we would walk down and back on the mats doing a handstand. We did not have any excuses for not trying, because we would get to see Floyd Winter do it prior to us.

After warmups, we would do par terre shadow wrestling defense. Floyd would yell, "Circle left, circle right, forward, he's trying to lift you, MOVE!" Sometimes it felt like we would do this for 20 minutes. Then we practiced drilling techniques. After this we would live pummel for about thirty minutes, switching partners every minute. It did not matter if you wrestled 105 pounds or 220 pounds, you would pummel with everyone. While we were pummeling, Floyd would yell, "Keep your hips *in,* don't let him drive you back, *circle.*" After this we would end morning practice with 200 push-ups and 200 sit-ups.

All Army afternoon practices started with cross training again. Gymnastics, jogging, and pummeling. After this we would go through the par terre drills, live pummeling, and then live three- or four-man groups for about one hour. This is where you wrestle on your feet with everyone in your group, one minute or two minutes each, rotating until the hour ended.

Then we would do live groups in the par terre position, 30 second rotations for about 30 minutes. This was followed by partner weight training. You would do partner body curls, picking your partner up off the mat chest high, flipping them over, placing their feet on the opposite side, pop ups, and pummeling with the weights. After this we had my favorite part of practice. Imagery, relaxation, and Floyd Winter's motivational speech. It started out like this…

In the ancient Greek Olympic Games, there were only three combative sports. Wrestling, boxing, and pankration. The pankration was the most dangerous and difficult of all the Olympics Sports. It was a combination of wrestling and boxing. It was often a fight to the death. There were only three ways to leave the arena; dead, surrender draped over your comrade's shoulders in defeat, or carried out victorious. One of the most legendary pankration athletes was in his 21st straight Olympic Games without one single defeat.

In ancient Greece, the Olympics were every year. This year the aging pankration Champion faced a younger, stronger, and more robust opponent. Everyone was sure the aging pankration Champion would be defeated this time. As the battle progressed, the young athlete rang blow after blow upon him, but the aging Champion would not surrender.

The young athlete began to grapple and placed the aging pankration Champion in a deadly choke hold. The great aging Champion reached out, grasped the ankle of the younger warrior, and twisted it until it broke. The younger pankration athlete surrendered, while the great aging Champion pitched forward dead in the dust of the arena. He is the only man in the history of the ancient Greek Olympics to receive the Laurel Reef posthumously (at the same time of his death). This aging Champion showed what mental courage and toughness really was.

A higher form of *mental courage* is a soldier who, while in combat, facing an enemy ambush, throws himself on an enemy grenade without hesitation to save the lives of his squad members. I once knew a man who did just that and lived. However, the odds are against you. For his troubles, he received the Medal of Honor, the highest award a soldier can receive in combat.

Floyd would tell us, "In order to be successful wrestlers we must have the mental courage to run the miles, to lift those weights, and practice if we want to be champions."

Floyd Winter's strength was his ability to motivate and train wrestlers with little to no Greco-Roman experience to become Armed Forces and National Champions. He was able to take inexperienced Army soldiers and turn us into Armed Forces and National Greco–Roman wrestling Champions. Some examples are Randy Couture, Derrick Waldroup, Martin Strmiska, Romey Pelletier, myself and many others.

Each year in U.S. Army Europe we would have USAEUR wrestlers, coaches and official Clinics. In 1985 I was attending the USAEUR Wrestlers Clinic. When Floyd arrived, he told me, "Tony instead of going to the wrestlers and coaches clinic you should attend the officials clinic." I did not understand, but he explained to me in order to be a great wrestler you have to understand the rules from the official's point of view.

At that time, I did not understand, but during the 1988 National Wrestling Championship Semifinal I began to understand. During the Semifinal match at the 163 pounds weight class I was in a 0–0 match with the defending National Champion, David Butler. Late in the match, with the score tied, the official put up the sign issuing a double disqualification for David Butler and I.

In the heat of the moment I stated, "Let us finish the match!" Floyd yelled from the corner, "No Tony, be quiet!" I came to the corner after the double disqualification. I asked Coach, "Why didn't you let us finish the match?" He stated, "Congratulations, you are in the finals. You have the most points from all the previous matches wrestled in the tournament."

Because of Floyd Winter's strategy and understanding of the rules I was able to win the 1988 National Greco-Roman Championship. Several times during my coaching career I was able to win matches for my wrestlers. This was because of Floyd sending me to the official's clinic and showing me the importance of understanding the wrestling rules and strategies.

Floyd Winter selected me to replace him as the All Army Wrestling Coach in 1989. I coached the All Army Team from 1989 through 1996. He mentored me throughout my coaching career, often calling and advising me on what to do and how to get the best out of the All Army Wrestlers. I used all the plans he developed for practice. I used everything from the sprints, long distance runs, gymnastics, live three- or four-man groups, to the discipline that he taught me my first year. Floyd's system is the reason the All Army Team was able to win every Armed Forces Championship from 1990 through 1996, place wrestlers on the 1992 and 1996 Olympic Team, and produce an Olympic Bronze Medal.

~ Tony Thomas
Hometown: Milledgeville, GA
All Army Wrestler 1983–1988
All Army and WCAP Wrestling Coach 1989–1996
Retired USA Army Cavalry Scout, Army rank Sergeant First Class
1984 AAU National Sombo Champion
1988 USA Wrestling National Greco-Roman Champion
1994 USA Wrestling National Coach of the Year
1996 USA Espoir/ University Leader of the Year

I met Coach Winter at Rose Barracks in Bad Kreuznach, Germany in the Fall of 1977, when he served as the visiting clinician at the United States Army European (USAREUR) wrestling clinic. As a civilian sports specialist with the Army, my role was to organize and administer the clinic, while Floyd taught skills and techniques to coaches and soldier-wrestlers.

Although I knew little about him, his legend preceded him. I was told not to worry, that he was a great clinician. Little did I know how good he was.

I was also told that he had previously been assigned to a unit at Rose Barracks, and this was his first trip back to Bad Kreuznach since previously being assigned there. Although I learned that he was the first American to win a Greco-Roman Gold medal in world competition, when he won the 1972 World Military Wrestling Championships in Ankara, Turkey, I could not appreciate what that meant.

Floyd told me that he learned about Greco-Roman wrestling during his previous assignment in Bad Kreuznach. While assigned there, he would travel to Mainz to train with a German wrestling club. This is where he learned about Greco-Roman, how champions were made, and how friendships were formed.

At that time, Greco-Roman seemed about as foreign as the country in which I was living. My boss, the Fifth Corps Sports Director, had given me the challenge of overseeing wrestling in the nine military communities that comprised Fifth Corps. The rules portion of the clinic was led by a civilian with the Air Force stationed in Wiesbaden. Wrestling was growing in USAREUR.

Floyd was well-received by the coaches and wrestlers and was invited back again the following year. Joining him this time from the states was Dr. Vince Zuaro who served as the rules clinician. All I knew about Dr. Zuaro was that he was a lifetime educator from Long Island who was also the editor of the rule book. Again, little did I know.

In time I learned that Dr. Zuaro had founded the U.S. Wrestling Officials Association and had spent his life educating and training wrestling officials. By the time he hung up his whistle, Dr. Zuaro had officiated in five Olympic Games, 34 World Championships, six Pan American Championships, and 30 years of national tournaments.

Three times Dr. Zuaro was presented the highest award of international wrestling, as well as the Gold Whistle, symbolic for being the top official in Olympic and World officiating. And yet, it was clear that Dr. Zuaro considered it an honor to be spending time with soldiers stationed in Europe.

They were such a hit, that for several years, the clinician-team of Winter and Zuaro would spend a week with wrestlers, coaches, and officials. The week always ended with a tournament during which both the wrestlers and officials could put their skills to the test. Soldiers came from throughout Europe to learn and wrestle.

Each year the Armed Forces Network would broadcast a report on the clinic. The Stars and Stripes newspaper would interview Floyd and Dr. Zuaro, and would publish a lengthy story on the clinic. Often, the two clinicians would meet with some of the top commanders. They were greatly admired and respected by everyone.

They stayed in the VIP quarters, were featured on television and in the newspaper, and spent each evening dining and drinking beer with some of the attendees at a different gasthaus or restaurant each night. Although they had achieved some level of notoriety, they were always humble and giving.

These times proved to be more important than the wrestling itself. Wrestling became a place where lifelong friendships were formed.

Floyd would entertain everyone at dinner with stories from his travels to Iran and different countries. He said he was "multilingual," which meant he could order beer in several different languages. However, his real universal language was card tricks.

Whenever someone gave him a deck of cards, he would dazzle everyone with one card trick after another. His delivery was always with a deadpan look on his face, and some doubt about whether or not it was even doable. He would say, "I don't know if I can do this. I haven't done it in a long time." Or, "This has never been done before." Of course, he always pulled it off and left everyone gasping and laughing out loud. He was the master of suspense, and seldom paid for his beer.

After being stationed in Berlin, he created the Freedom Cup Wrestling Tournament, featuring teams representing Denmark, Germany, Turkey, and the United States Army in Europe. The Germans and the Americans had excellent relationships, and since Floyd had taken a team of soldiers to Denmark for a tournament, the Danes reciprocated by traveling to Berlin. The Turkish team was another story.

The tournament was attended by several high-ranking personnel to include an ambassador, representatives of the Consulate General, and several commanders. The evening had all of the pomp and circumstances associated with an important international tournament.

As one of the mat officials during the Freedom Cup, I gave a Turkish wrestler his second caution for stalling, which meant he was very close to being disqualified. Angered at the call, the Turkish coach came onto the mat and told me in broken English that he would immediately take his entire team from the gym if his wrestler was cautioned-out. We managed to finish the match without anyone being cautioned-out, in spite of the challenge.

Following the tournament, all of the participants gathered at the Harnack House for a festive celebration with food and drink. Taken by the Americans in 1945 as the war drew to a close, the Harnack House served as an American military hotel and Officers Club. Amazingly, Floyd had managed to bring people together from four countries as he demonstrated the ideal of friendship through sports.

The following day, when looking at a photo album at Floyd's apartment, I noticed a picture of the Turkish coach playing third base in one of Floyd's softball games. Until then, I did not realize that the two of them were friends, which is how the Turkish team came to be in the Freedom Cup. Once again, the ease with which Floyd made friends was evident.

While stationed in Berlin, Floyd continued to mine the gyms for talent that he could bring into the All Army Training Camp for wrestling. Once he had them in camp, he would put them on a path to becoming national and international champions.

In 1985, I became the Sports Director at Fort Campbell, Kentucky. As Floyd was completing his assignment at West Point, we talked about him possibly being assigned to Fort Campbell and conducting the All Army Wrestling Trial Camp at the home of the 101st Airborne Division.

He arrived for duty at Fort Campbell in 1986 and was assigned to the Community Recreation Division, Sports Branch. At that point, I became his supervisor.

He went to work as soon as he arrived, selecting athletes, preparing for their arrival, securing lodging, arranging for mats, and meeting commanders. One day, when dressed in his Army uniform, he was told that he was not authorized to display the insignia for the German Parachute Badge on his uniform. To his chagrin, he had to take off his German Jump Wings.

He conducted the All Army Wrestle-Offs and the team flew to Mather Air Force Base in California for the Armed Forces Championships. The Marines continued their winning ways over the Army, but the writing was on the wall.

Floyd managed to keep as many team members as possible at Fort Campbell as they continued to train in Greco-Roman. He knew that the only way to get better was through experience. He made it his goal for the team to participate in as many competitions as possible.

He traveled to California and Michigan for tournaments, as well as USA Wrestling's National Championships. Every time he returned to Fort Campbell he would conduct a trophy presentation to the Commanding General, who took great pride in seeing the success of the soldiers.

In 1988, the Armed Forces Championships were held at Fort Campbell and the Army beat the Marines. Again, this was no small accomplishment. Floyd arranged for Gary Kurdelmeir, the former Iowa Wrestling Coach and then Executive Director of USA Wrestling, to speak at the closing banquet. It seemed as if Floyd knew everyone.

Floyd did not know everyone, but he could talk to anyone. Humbleness and humility were his trademarks, and respect was his calling card. He also came back from competitions with T-shirts and memorabilia that he shared with the Fort Campbell staff.

By the time he retired from active duty in 1989, he had done it all, from selecting and training the team, to writing policy letters and rolling out the mats.

The Army Wrestling Team became the team to beat in the Armed Forces Championships. Throughout it all, he never lost his love for wrestling and people he met along the way. Floyd had friends from across the world.

The Army is about combat, and wrestling is a combative sport. Floyd knew that wrestling for the All Army Team was a privilege, and not a right. His challenge was to help each competitor to rise to his highest possible skill level. He also knew that they had to have fun in the process.

As Army wrestlers came onto the mat, it was easy to see the heart and mind of the American soldier. Floyd made them winners, and after wrestling with Coach Winter, they were confident that they could handle almost anything in their careers.

~ Van Stokes

I first met Coach Winter in February of 2013. The United States Air Force, ALL Air Force Team (Greco-Roman/Freestyle) had come to train at Joint Base McGuire-Dix-Lakehurst for camp. It consisted of a few phases. First you had to be invited to Camp, second you had to wrestle off for your spot on the team and then next was the U.S. Armed Forces Championship (which is a U.S. World Team & Olympic Team Trials qualifier) and then on to the U.S. Open/Greco/Freestyle National Championship.

They had set up shop on the Fort Dix side of the base. It just so happened they signed the training facility out that used to be where I had spent a few years training the Modern Army Combative Instructors in Brazilian Jiu-Jitsu & Catch Wrestling. So, I knew the level 4 MACP Instructors very well.

Now talk about bad timing. I had right knee surgery in November and in mid-January I had my left biceps reattached, my left collarbone cut completely through to get it to drop back down into place and my left torn labrum fixed all in one miserable day at the University of Pennsylvania Hospital in Philly.

So now it has been months since I've been lifting weights, running, or grappling. My Army instructor buddies kept leaving voicemails on my phone for about three straight days. On my first day back to work on base I finally called the guys back. They informed me the USAF All Air Force Team was training on base and they felt their Heavyweights would be no match for me.

Now keep in mind, my wrestling background was some Folkstyle from private lessons with a Division 1 Heavyweight All American out of Ohio who came to New Jersey, and Legendary Coach Billy Robinson in Catch

Wrestling. Other than that, I was on the verge of my Brazilian Jiu-Jitsu Black Belt and Judo Black Belt having started those back in early 1998.

I showed up to the room (with my sling on and still bruised from the surgeries) and introduced myself to the then coach named Rich. Immediately he informed me that not only was I insane because of the surgeries and still showing up just a few weeks after having them, but to try to wrestle All Americans and even Senior National Champions was nuts.

Rich was the only American coach to win a World Championship in Greco Roman history. I was impressed, of course, but I wanted to know how in the world I could be a part of this special opportunity and team.

I told him I had packed a bag for a workout and maybe he could just take a look. He reluctantly agreed, obviously because of all the recent surgeries which were far from healed. I am sure he did not want to be responsible for me tearing apart all of what had been repaired, especially down the left side of my torso.

I beat every heavyweight out for the spot but I needed help. Greco and Freestyle were new to me. I had a great front headlock and outside single. I used that same front headlock to get my turns on the ground to rack up points because I was not familiar with all the leg laces or gut wrenches for the purpose of turns. To be honest, I had to duct tape my left arm to my body around my biceps/triceps area to keep the surgeries from being undone. Although I never thought of it at the time, I'm sure the fellas had a hard time getting an underhook on that side.

Rich called up a man who was the Team Manager at the time. He walked into the room one day and there he was,

Coach Floyd "Bad News" Winter. He came across humble, kind, and generous. Characteristics I had never trusted at first due to my upbringing in a violent home. I never really had a father figure or a real man to take me under his wing.

Coach Winter did private lessons with me every day Monday through Friday. Then after that season three or four times a week at lunch as well as with a coworker of mine. He was a great wrestler out of University of Pennsylvania a few years back and had served as an EOD in the Navy. His name was Jon Gough and without him there would not have been any workouts, at least at this point.

So, I am 35 and the oldest guy on the team with a lot more miles on my body than your average 35-year-old. To explain it a bit further I was labeled as a completely and totally disabled Vet shortly after I retired at 38. Floyd did not care; he saw something in me. He was such a master motivator and leader I would do anything he asked without thinking twice. I wrestled for the team one more year only because they fired the other coach and asked Floyd to come back. No way I could miss this chance to actually wrestle for him. Then I spent two more years as one of his assistant coaches for the team. Rich was an amazing technician but not a coach. Floyd was both.

Between seasons we started not just training, but hanging out at lunchtime in his office where he was the Athletic Director for the entire joint base. I would bring him lunch and we would just talk. Over time he became one of my best friends and eventually the father figure I had never had. I never sought that from him, it just happened…

My daughter Alexandria came with me to Floyd's office. She always liked him. She was probably five or six at the time and Coach asked her about how she is doing in school or something like that. She responded, "I have straight A's!" Coach said, "Well then, you deserve an award." He reached up above his shelf and grabbed the first trophy he touched, not even knowing what it was. He hands it to her and says "Congratulations! Just keep doing great!" I was floored…it was from the German Wrestling Championships in the early 1970s, for first place, and was about half as big as her. She was so excited! To this day she keeps it on her nightstand.

I tried to stop him but that was just how he was. He literally gave me the shirt off his back, outside in the cold winter, from a camp we did together when I joked about not getting one. There is and will always be only ONE Floyd Winter.

I happily managed and organized his retirement ceremony and made him a Head Coach in my Organization "Snake Pit U.S.A. Catch Wrestling Association."

All four of my kids and wife adore him and his amazing wife Paula. I never became that All American he thought I could, regardless of my age. For years I felt I had failed him.

He was the one who never gave up on me. He knew I was not a quitter; I had been through some of the most rigorous courses the military had to offer and was a three-time Operation Enduring Freedom (Afghanistan) vet and one-time Operation Iraqi Freedom vet on top of a couple other Middle Eastern trips. I had spent over 1000 days and nights in the ICBM missile fields, living there day and night away from family. Maybe that mental toughness and similar military experience we shared joined us in some way, I do not know.

Floyd Winter (left) and Joel Bane in front of Tom Jenkins' portrait at West Point. Jenkins was a former Catch Wrestling World Heavyweight Champion and the Military's first Combative Instructor. He taught at West Point for 37 years. He taught Patton, Eisenhower, and many more Catch Wrestling and Boxing.

Floyd Winter (left) and Joel Bane at a Catch Wrestling seminar hosted by Snake Pit U.S.A.

Being with Floyd on those mats and becoming friends with him were the highlights of my Military career. He is and will always be to me the Father I never had. My wife says the same about him. He is the most wonderful human I have ever had the privilege of knowing. I love the man and so does my entire family and Team Snake Pit U.S.A.!

I love ya, Coach! Thank you for EVERYTHING!

~ Joel Bane
Head Coach
Snake Pit U.S.A. Catch Wrestling Association
www.SnakePitUSA.com

I first met Coach Floyd Winter when he was stationed in Berlin, West Germany at a U.S. Army Sports Director's meeting. At the time he was the volunteer Berlin wrestling coach for the Berlin Brigade. It was in the late 1970s and during the Cold War. The Berlin Wall did not come down until 1989 and Berlin was considered as isolated.

Floyd used to laugh and tell me that the Turkish women in Berlin who served as janitors all knew him through wrestling. He always got smiles when he was running the steps to maintain his fitness as they were cleaning. Floyd either was on Turkish wrestling teams or wrestled against them and the women all watched him when they went to those international matches. Winter did not have a lot of officials for the matches so I know Van Stokes traveled to Berlin to assist Floyd during those days. Van told me it was an experience he would never forget refereeing those international matches.

In the late 1970s, Coach Winter was lobbying the seven sports directors serving in Germany in attendance for Berlin, his garrison to host the event. To me it was a no brainer to accept his offer to host since he was the current All Army wrestling coach and All Army wrestler.

Floyd had more experience than all the attendees in the conference room. The vote was unanimous 7–0 and that Winter and all the teams totaling over one hundred Soldier-Athletes rode the military duty train from Frankfurt through East Germany to the island city of Berlin. Berlin was completely surrounded by the country of East Germany and guarded by the East German and Russian Soldiers. The bad news was during the actual event, the Army sent Floyd somewhere on a mission and he was not present during the event.

Floyd's team had the fewest number of soldiers on the team and the fewest number of soldiers to select from. All the other six teams had thousands of soldiers to select from and Floyd's team fewer than 2,000 because of the military structure in Germany. Floyd's team won the most gold medals in that U.S. Army Europe Freestyle and Greco tournament that championship.

Floyd coached the Berlin team and they were simply better trained. The match was covered by the Armed Forces Radio and Television Services (AFN), Stars & Stripes, and the Berlin Brigade newspaper. I made the comment to the Stars and Stripes sportswriter that "My team is dropping like flies." It was true but not appreciated by my coach. This was the beginning of a relationship that would last until this day.

When my team members wrestled against Floyd himself, they came off with a loss and said, "Wrestling against Floyd Winter is like tying up against a gyroscope." Once Winter locked with his opponent he knew which foot his opponent had the most weight on and/or if his opponent had his weight on his heels or toes. Then it was just a matter of seconds before Winter would take them to the mat, and then to their backs, and eventually pin them.

I refereed some of Winter's matches in those days and his wife Paula was there for his home matches and at mat-side hollering and encouraging him. Paula was never shy.

It was estimated that one third of the All Army wrestling team advancing from Europe made the team. The All Army Team went on to compete in the Armed Forces Wrestling Free Style and Greco-Roman Championships. Soldiers wrestled for both German clubs as well as for their military garrison teams.

And in two sports boxing and wrestling, there was one or more nationally ranked military amateur athletes in each weight class. The military teams always were a force in Greco-Roman wrestling. In those days, Folkstyle or Freestyle were the wrestling disciplines in high school and college wrestling. Fewer than a thousand wrestlers in America competed in Greco that led to the Olympics. That gave the upper hand to military athletes who focused on Greco-Roman and Floyd was the expert coach.

At that time, I did not know it but Coach Floyd had won the first gold medal competing at the World Military Championships (CISM) or (Council of International Military) hosted in the Middle East. Floyd always had a story.

He told me about running in the deserts at night when he was training. He could hear the dogs howling and he said it was kind of scary. And when his opponents stepped on the mat to compete, the fans would shout "Allah Akbar" and "Allah Ekber" an Islamic phrase, meaning "God is greater" or "God is greatest." Floyd still won. And the next day when walking in the streets Floyd was recognized and a familiar face from the competition the previous day on local TV. In the Middle East wrestling is their #1 sport like soccer is in Germany or England.

1980 was Floyd's year to compete in the Olympics. He was at the top of his game and he had qualified. After so many years of training and competing he had qualified to represent the USA in the Summer Olympics. Then President Jimmy Carter boycotted it. He and thousands of USA athletes were denied an opportunity that comes along only once in a lifetime. After Floyd did go to the Olympics, but only as a trainer or coach.

When Floyd was no longer wrestling, and serving as a coach or tournament director, I was on the mat as an official. He would wait till my match was complete and provide me with constructive criticism and tips to make me a better referee.

Later, Floyd was retired and working a civilian sports and fitness director job at Wiesbaden, Germany. Floyd called and asked me to come to Wiesbaden and assist him with youth wrestling tournaments as a mat official in which I continue to do until this day.

While at Wiesbaden he hosted the Department of Defense (DODDs) and Child and Youth Services (CYS) wrestling championships. That has been 20 plus years ago and still to this day the championships are still conducted in Wiesbaden. In the DODDs event teams from as far away as Ankara, Turkey, Italy, England, Belgium, and Germany compete for three or four days to determine their high school boys and girls champions. This is a long program that Coach Winter started that has stood the test of time.

Floyd ran one of the toughest camps in the military. One of my top military wrestlers who wrestled on my team from Wurzburg, Germany and the 3rd Infantry Division was Capt. Charles (Chuck) Africano. He won his weight division at 180.5 pounds, I believe. He went back for one of Coach Floyd's training camps and when he returned, he was 149 pounds.

Africano said it was the toughest military training he had ever gone through. And Africano graduated from Ranger training. Ranger students conduct about *20 hours of training per day,* while consuming two or fewer meals daily totaling about 2,200 calories (9,200 kJ), with an average of three-and-a-half hours of sleep a day. Students sleep more before a parachute jump for safety considerations.

In the early 1990s five events took place that changed and reshaped the U.S. Army sports and wrestling program. Floyd Winter retired as coach of the Army wrestling program and Tony Thomas who wrestled for Floyd took over the reins. Brigadier General John G. (Gil) Myers became the director of the division that provided the overall leadership and breathed life into the World Class Athlete Program (WCAP). He was crazy about sports and funded the program with a staff of three and gave them monies for travel, training, and equipment. The goal of this program was any soldier-athlete who had the skills and chance of making the Olympic team could be assigned to this elite sports program.

The final event was the program was moved from Ft. Benning, Georgia to Ft. Carson, Colorado directly under the nose of the U.S. Olympic Committee and the Headquarters of the National Government Body of Wrestling. So, if the new coach Tony Thomas wanted to train with the elite civilian wrestlers they could just drive a few miles to the Olympic training center. If the Army needed a medical doctor or physiologist they were free and available. WCAP staff members could go out on site and assist where needed. Before, the entire Army Sports Staff was run by two members, now they had five.

In former times even when the Armed Forces Sports Wrestling Championship was conducted at Quantico, Virginia, often called the crossroads of the Marine Corps, the two Army staff members did not have time to even attend the event. Now a staff member was there for the daily competition. The results were dynamic. Two wrestlers, Specialist Rodney Smith and Staff Sergeant Derrick Waldroup made the 1996 U.S.A. Olympic team hosted at Atlanta, Ga. So, after Floyd Winter three people plus a general officer assisted in a program that he was trying to run by himself.

Never turn down an opportunity to get Coach Floyd Winter as speaker for your sports event. He was inspiring to the attendees and spoke without notes. He spoke about what it took to be a champion. He provided examples on how to win. He talked of running over one more hill, running one more mile; doing five more pushups and pullups; and ten more stomach crunches.

He provided examples of Olympic swimming events where races are won and lost by less than a second. His speeches were those of the Olympics; Faster, Higher and Stronger. Soldiers like Randy Couture heard those speeches and went on to be idols in MMA. Rodney Smith heard those speeches and won a bronze medal in the 1992 Olympics in Barcelona, Spain. Only hard work and dedication will get you there on the gold medal platform.

Over Floyd's lifetime, he has impacted any and everyone in the sport of wrestling. He has impacted youth, high schoolers, and military grapplers. He has directed or assisted in the conduct of the Olympic, Military, World Military (CISM), high school and youth championships. There is no wrestling event Coach Floyd Winter has not been involved in, either as a wrestler, official, or administrator.

~ Tom Hlavacek

I first met Floyd in Germany when I was wrestling in a European Championship. I did not know him from a hill of beans. Someone said there is a guy here who recruits from the All Army Team. I did not really pay attention to it, just wrestled and did well in the tournament.

He came up to me, I think it was in 1980, and asked me if I would like to wrestle for the All Army Team. I told him I was not familiar with it. He said that he needed a good heavyweight and that he could work with me.

I did not know Greco very well; I was more of a Freestyle guy. He talked me into it. It was tough getting me out to wrestle for the All Army Team. When you are an officer it is a major challenge to get away.

Floyd would write these letters to get me out. He would not write them to my immediate supervisor. He would write them to the Commanding General, which would sometimes make my supervisors mad. Every year he wrote a letter for me to get me out of command.

I was a tac helicopter pilot. I was the biggest pilot in the Army as a matter of fact. I flew cobra gunships for the border patrol in Germany. I had to get a waiver to fly and they did not have a uniform that fit me. When I would sit in the cockpit my calves would come through my uniform. They flew me to Philadelphia and put me on a table to sketch out how big my uniform should be. They had to make a helmet for me too because I have a big head.

Floyd would write these letters. The first sentence or two would grab the commander or general's attention. It basically said that because of their jobs they may not know some of the talents inside their agency or someone who may need to be recognized.

Floyd would put all his credentials on there and they were very impressive of course. I would always get a call directly from the General. Here I am a lowly Captain or Lieutenant getting a call from the higher ups. They would tell me, "You are released. Now go and try to make the Olympic Team!"

He wrote these letters for a couple of us, and it really worked. It was tough for the officers because we always had to go back. As a pilot I had to keep current in the aircraft. Sometimes I had to leave early because of military operations. Sometimes I got to stay for the All Army stuff. I would go to Nationals and train for the Pan American games and try out for the Olympic Team. All of that was because of Floyd Winter. He is just an incredible guy.

Most of us who wrestled with Floyd talk about having PTSD from his whistle. Floyd would blow that whistle nonstop. He was big into cardio training. So, we ran probably five miles worth of 50 yard dashes, 100 yard dashes, 220s and 880s. We would do a run after that and go right into wrestling practice. That whistle just blew nonstop.

When we were inside the wrestling room a couple of us would try to steal his whistle. We would take the ball out of it and all kinds of stuff. He would always have a backup whistle. That was one of the biggest things we would always talk about when we got together as a team was that whistle blowing. I played college football and I am used to all that stuff, but Floyd just knew how to blow that whistle.

I was an Army Ranger and was used to running even though I was big. I went back to Germany for a PT test. It was the first time I ever ran a 13-minute two mile. I was probably 285 pounds. That was because of Floyd's sprints and whistle.

We were at Fort Bliss. Floyd was blowing his whistle and we had guys throwing up on the track. We ran the stairs in stadiums until people were puking. There were a couple of guys who came over to us and said that they wanted to join the All Army Track Team. We had our All Army sweats on. They thought we were on the track team because they saw us running so much!

The heavyweights were running like elephants around the track and all the little guys were passing us about every minute or so.

Everyone knows me by the name of "Big Hands." Floyd gave me that name, most people do not even know my real name. Floyd led by example. He had to come out of retirement in 1981 and wrestle. Floyd came up to me and said, "Big Hands, you are hurting all the guys in the upper weight classes! I'm getting concerned. I don't know if they are going to heal in time or not."

Everybody was getting hurt back then. We were just wrestling and training hard. But he had to come out of retirement because too many wrestlers were hurt. We were training at West Point at the time. It was just an amazing thing; we were at an Interservice Tournament at Quantico and everybody was watching this guy come out of retirement.

He looked like he was not in shape, but when we were training at West Point he was running all the sprints with us. It was incredible. He was gassing on his runs but he finally hit his stride and he was training hard with us. He ended up winning that tournament in 1981. When Floyd won that, the place went nuts! Everybody was there just to watch Floyd wrestle. It was amazing.

When it came to us as a team, he took care of us so well. He has never forgotten us. He was big into camaraderie. He has had to fight for us so many times. He really had challenges getting the All Army Wrestling Team off the ground. There were budget issues and nobody understood why we should have an Army Wrestling Team, even though we had an Army Boxing Team.

He would have to fight the Department of Army for funding. It took money to keep the program going. He also had to fight folks when we would train at West Point, Fort Dix, Fort Bliss, and Fort Campbell. A lot of the higher ups did not understand what we were doing even though we were soldiers too. Sometimes it was tough getting things organized as far as equipment and places to workout. For example, taking over a gym that the soldiers probably wanted to play basketball in, things like that.

It was also a good recruiting tool for the Army because a lot of people saw us. We had Olympians, World Champions, National Champions etc. A lot of soldiers would see us and if they wrestled in high school or college they would want to join the All Army Team. We ended up getting some premier athletes out of that.

I wrestled for the University of Toledo. I had a friend there, Greg Wojciechowski, the great Wojo. He was on the Olympic Team and a World Champion. That is probably the first guy I pummeled with and he asked me to do some Greco-Roman wrestling with him. I was not big into Greco.

He was on the 1980 Olympic Team. Wojciechowski also beat the famous Chris Taylor. I ended up wrestling him and another guy who was there from Bulgaria and he was a bronze medalist. That was my eye opener that I was going to have to step up my game as a wrestler because these guys were just incredible.

Floyd wrestled Wojciechowski. I did not know that until years later. One day Wojciechowski's name came up and Floyd's eyes lit up. He said, "I've wrestled him!" Floyd was at the Michigan Open. At the last second he was told to wrestle up two weight classes. Floyd was only 198 pounds and had to wrestle the huge Wojciechowski at heavyweight. And he won! His next time wrestling Wojo he lost in the last segment due to a contested call. Wojciechowski had a friend named Dick Torreo who knew all the referees and also ran a gymnasium for wrestling in Toledo. Dick knew the ref and came down and was screaming that Floyd's throw was not legal and he should not have gotten the three points. The three points were taken away from Floyd and he ended up losing the match.

I already really respected Floyd but when he tells you those type of things it is just really amazing. He wrestled and won against guys I thought were unbeatable. Floyd was always the guy who was smaller. Wojciechowski is huge, he is not a small guy.

Floyd loved to be with the guys, his wrestlers. He kept us under control so we did not do anything stupid. He had to go fight for one soldier who was going to lose his career for doing something stupid. It was not during the wrestling season; it was before he came back on the wrestling team.

Floyd had to put his Class As on and speak to the board. He fought for this soldier and got him reinstated so he could continue his career in the Army. That is why we have another good officer in the Army, because of what Floyd did. Floyd has a lot of contacts and if you ever need help he knows who to go to. He is just amazing and I cannot say enough about the guy.

Most of the wrestlers who came into the program were Freestyle or Folkstyle. They had to be taught Greco-Roman wrestling, which is tough. Then, all of a sudden, Floyd threw Sambo in there at us! That was back in the early 1980s. We had never heard of Sambo before. One day a guy shows up with a Judo jacket on and Floyd says, "We are going to train to be Sambo wrestlers too." He showed us jacket wrestling and we won two National Titles in that. I ended up being a National Champion.

Floyd got me on the Pan Am team. Greco got me to the final trials in the Olympics. I lost to Blatnick who went on to win the Olympics. Floyd ended up helping coach Blatnick in the Olympics and I think he really helped him get over the top and win.

Floyd played a lot of Vietnam Era music during wrestling practice. Every day it was the same songs over and over again. That and his whistle blowing gave us all PTSD! The music was not for some of the younger guys.

I owe Floyd so much for getting me to the World Championships, helping me win the National Title, and a bronze medal in the World Games in London. All of that was because of Floyd Winter. I will always remember him for that.

~ Gary "Big Hands" Barber

I started coaching wrestling in high school. Then I coached at the University of California in Berkley. I got involved with the National Program and I was the President of the Coaches Association. I became involved with Greco-Roman Wrestling because Freestyle has always been the one most people were interested in. I figured Greco needed some help.

I was the president and we had a meeting. I said, "Okay, guys we're going to have a Greco tournament. Who wants to do it?" Nobody wanted to do it. So, I thought, "Okay, Goddamnit, I'll do it!" I went overseas and contacted the coaches and their presidents. I told them we were going to host an invitational tournament in Concord, California.

To my surprise we had fourteen countries come to the first tournament. We ran the Concord Cup Tournament for the next 21 years. It was essentially a grass roots program. We really had no support and just hustled our own money. It was a very popular tournament and the countries kept wanting to come back.

That tournament became *the Greco-Roman tournament*. Primarily because it was the only one of its kind and secondarily because we had all the best countries coming. Russia came every year and Japan and all the big players in Greco. Out of that tournament we were also able to start a wrestling club for the kids. We opened that up and ran it for about 20 years.

My wife Betty always was a sports fan and she was a good hostess for all the countries. We had a lot of nice parties and receptions at our house.

Floyd was the coach of the Army Team. The services of the Air Force, Navy, Army, and Marines were always big sponsors of wrestling. All the services always came to my tournament. That is how I met Floyd.

Floyd and I became good friends because we were both interested in Greco. Floyd was real, there was no pretense with him. We were the primary instigators for tournaments. We did everything from setting up mats, to clinics, and hosting tournaments. When teams would come here for the Concord Tournament we would take them and tour around the Bay area and host competitions with local clubs.

It actually turned into a pretty big deal. The wrestling club is still there but after 21 years when I retired no one jumped in my shoes for the Concord Cup. It died after that.

It was a great tournament though. Since we had pretty much all of the medalists here from Greco we decided we should showcase these guys. So, prior to the tournament we had what we called the "Gold Medal Match" at the local Hilton Hotel.

We had the American Champions compete against all the medal winners from the foreign countries. We would host this match in the ballroom at the hotel. That turned out to be a very popular event. We had some great wrestling there. The Gold Medal Match turned out to be one of the main attractions every year.

It was because of guys like Floyd who would come in early with his team and help set things up, do tours, promotions, and newspaper interviews that the event was so successful. It turned out to be an essentially Floyd Winter & Bill Martel Tournament. *Floyd and I were Greco-Roman wrestling for many years.*

~ Bill Martel

I am just a simple guy who played football at Yukon and got a teaching job right outside of Yukon. Around 1980 this woman told me I should go teach overseas with the Department of Defense. I went to Germany and taught for 23 years.

I met Floyd a long time ago. I had read his bio before I ever met him. I was really taken aback by how he came to me, a high school teacher/coach, and treated me like his equal. He just wanted to help out. He is a very giving man.

He did things for free all the time. He got to know the German wrestlers too and did things for free for them as well. We would have clinics that he and I put on with the American and German kids for free.

Through the years we became really good friends. He was also one of the best referees. We did the European finals together and he was excellent.

Getting back to Floyd as a person, he always had the best interest of other people at heart. He did not wear his wrestling accolades on his shoulder. He was just a super fun guy to be around.

He came to me one day and said, "How would you like to hold the European Finals?" The European Finals at the time had 32 high schools. It was a really big tournament that we would now be hosting and I was very excited about it.

We took it on, him and I. We arranged hotels and transportation and got some Colonels involved. We had lunches and dinners and this and that. We worked really hard at it, him more than I because I still had to teach and coach. We put on the best European Finals that I think anyone has ever seen in Europe since it started in 1944.

It was really well done. Floyd knew all that stuff from his past experiences, he knew the ins and outs. Of course, doing that together made us better friends, because we would keep drinking beer when we were done doing our thing! He loved "Hepeviesen" beer. It is German for wheat beer.

We got to meet so many people. We met the Mayor of Wiesbaden, Germany, and a German National Champion. He would introduce these people to me and make me feel as important as he was. It was really just a special time and I truly appreciate Floyd for that.

~ Daryl Schwartz

I met Floyd around 1985. I had just joined the Army. I had finished basic training and AIT and was headed to my duty station. At that particular time, you had to put in an application and tryout for the wrestling team. I did not go in the Army to wrestle but I didn't like my job too much. So, I figured I might as well try out for the wrestling team.

I put my application into the wrestling team and got accepted to tryout. I went to tryouts at West Point. I got to West Point and stayed in the open bay barracks with a lot of other wrestlers. We trained for about 45 days. At the end of that you would have a wrestle off to see who would make the team.

The whole time I did not know much about Greco-Roman Wrestling. I was a Junior College National Champion in Freestyle. At that time, the Army Team was really into Greco, but Freestyle, not so much.

Floyd was always telling me, "You should wrestle Greco, you should wrestle Greco." I kept telling him, "No coach, I'm a Freestyler, I don't wrestle Greco." He did this for the entire 45 days. At the end of the 45 days, we had wrestle offs and I ended up making the team. That let me stay a little bit longer.

I had made a deal with Floyd to try Greco. We wrestled in the Armed Forces and my first year I ended up winning the Greco and the Freestyle. After that I told Floyd, "That's it for me, no more Greco. I'm wrestling Freestyle!"

For the next month and a half that we trained, Floyd kept saying, "Just wrestle in the National Open, Just wrestle in the National Open in Greco." He said, "Just this one time, this year, and you won't have to do it anymore." I said, "Okay, Floyd, I'll wrestle in the Nationals in Greco." That year I won the Nationals in Greco. Floyd was right.

All the guys were hanging around afterword and one of the guys said, "Hey Derrick, you're going to wrestle Freestyle now right?" I looked at Floyd and Floyd looked at me. I said, "No, I don't wrestle Freestyle now, I'm a Greco wrestler!" Floyd had changed my mind.

I stayed in the Army for 15 more years. I wrestled every one of those 15 years. I ended up making the Olympic Team. I Wrestled in the 1996 Olympic Games. I won a World Military Championship and National Championships. I do not know what it was or how he did it, but Floyd could see it in a person. He could see a person and know, "Hey, that's a Greco wrestler." He had an eye for talent.

To tell you the truth, I did not think much about him at first. He just did not look like a typical wrestler; he did not have much muscle mass. But he would come in the room sometimes and walk across the entire mat on his hands.

After he started teaching I saw that he really knew his wrestling. He was very good at it; he knew the moves and the techniques. After every practice that first year, Floyd would come into the locker room and say, "Okay, who's going to the sauna with me and I'll tell you stories about the *'Nam*." At first, I never understood what the *'Nam* was.

After five or six months I understood it to be *Vietnam*. He was always like, "C'mon guys, let's go! Who's going to the sauna with me? I'm going to tell you some stories about 'Nam and Ho Chi Minh and the rice paddy fields!"

I always thought this guy was joking.

So, I started going to the sauna with him. He would tell us these stories about how they were on patrol through the rice paddy fields. Floyd was always a great storyteller. He had a knack for being able to remember every minute detail. It became kind of a ritual because I wanted to hear these stories. So, I started going to the sauna with him just to hear these stories.

He told stories from Vietnam and stories of Osamu Watanabe, one of the most decorated wrestlers in Olympic history. He just had all these stories! He could remember all of these stories and the details about them. He would tell us about walking in Vietnam through fields and the booby traps. Most of us were young, I was only 22 years old. I was thinking, "I don't think this guy has really ever been to Vietnam."

Every day we would pack into the sauna and listen to the stories. Later on, I found out that he was really in Vietnam. I did not really learn to have admiration for that until I worked for the VA. I spent 15 years working for the VA, adjudicating claims for veterans. I had to learn so much about Vietnam and the things that they went through to make it back home. As I grew older I was so impressed and grateful to have been able to hear some of those stories.

Every day for practice we came into the wrestling room and Floyd would have on 1960s music. He would be bebopping and jumping around. I thought, "Man, this guy is unusual." He always played 1960s R&B music. He knew all the words to the songs. I was from the city of Chicago, and it was just unusual for me to see an older white gentleman who knows all the R&B from the 1960s.

One day someone asked Floyd how he knew all this music. He said, "I was bedded down in a black regiment in Vietnam. Those guys kept me alive. This was the music they listened to all the time and I learned to love this music." He would always play it during practice and he called it, "Greco music."

Floyd's whistle and music were constant during training. The music was soothing, the whistle was not. He was very big on conditioning. I can remember one time he wanted us to come outside. There was a hill he made us run sprints on for 20 minutes, up and down. He said, "Okay. Overtime! Overtime! Get your buddy on your back!" You then had to get this big guy on your back and run up and down the hill. To be honest, I was not the most conditioned athlete. Floyd would always say that, "I was running with somebody else on my back plus a monkey." Because a monkey was always on my back because my conditioning was so bad. It was like a big gorilla would jump on my back and weigh me down, taking all my energy.

It is unfortunate that the wrestlers nowadays do not know the history of Army Wrestling. When you talk about the World Class Athlete Program (WCAP), Floyd was the one who built that. He made it possible for guys to leave their units and wrestle which was unheard of. Floyd Winter was the one who started all of this.

He had this uncanny knack to be able to go and talk to Generals. You join the Army to be a soldier. Your duties as a soldier came first. I have seen many, many times where a Commander says, "Nope, I'm not releasing this kid to go wrestle. We need him in the Unit." Lo and behold Floyd would say, "No worries, it's no problem. I'll take care of it." He would go and talk to Generals and Colonels and come back and say, "That soldier will be coming here to wrestle in a week or so." He could get guys out of Ranger Battalion. That is a very big deal. They never let anyone leave the Ranger Battalion.

When Floyd met a person and bonded with them he would never forget you. It could be 20 years later and he would be able to recall your name and when and where he met you. He never forgot a person.

The number of soldier-athlete's lives that he has touched is huge. He has touched a lot of human beings. My career, my success in life, on and off the mat, can all be attributed to Floyd and the lessons I learned from him.

~ Derrick Waldroup

I met Floyd back in 1977 when I was on the Berlin Boxing Team. I joined the team because I wanted to get into some sport that I had done before. I was also a State Wrestling Champion. While boxing I noticed these guys jumping around in the workout room on the mat. I thought, "Those guys have wrestling shoes on!" I threw my gloves off, jumped down on the mat, and said, "What's happening?"

Floyd responded, "I'm the wrestling coach." I told him, "Well, I'm a State Champion and I would like to join your team." So, I joined the Berlin Wrestling Team.

I then asked him, "What are you guys working out for?" Floyd replied, "To go for the Army Wrestling Team." I said, "Well, I want to join that too!" He told me I would have to win the European Championship. I said, "That's not a problem."

I went down to Italy with Floyd and won the European Championship. So, I earned the chance to go onto the Army Wrestling Team at West Point in 1977. I was on the Army Wrestling Team for two years in a row.

Floyd and I became really close, I even babysat his kids! He was an all-around good guy and we had some great times. I have never lost contact with Floyd since.

~ Venecom Griffin

I was a Lieutenant in Germany and I started wrestling in 1981. I was in a few tournaments and Floyd saw me. I was a pretty good wrestler and had won the USAREUR Championship.

Floyd told me I should wrestle for the Army. I made a deal with my command that I would do that for just one year. Floyd became my coach, but he was more than just a coach. The first year that I was on the Army Team he basically took me into his home. It was like a second home for me with him and Paula and their two kids.

After that I became an Executive Officer in an Air Defense Unit. I had all my MBT gear on, a mask and a suit. I was walking over to the Battalion Headquarters for a report.

This General Officers vehicle passed me and I saluted. It stopped at the headquarters. I walked into the Headquarters and I am screaming through my mask talking to someone. My Battalion Commander taps me on the shoulder. He is standing with this General Officer there. He tells me to come to attention.

Floyd had written a letter to the Division Commander. He told him that he thought I had the potential to make the U.S. Olympic Team. I just needed the opportunity to be able to do that. This is a year removed from me being on the All Army Team. My Commander had already told me that I was not going. This General Officer who came told me that they were willing to give me the chance.

Floyd got me out of Germany to wrestle. I would have never had the opportunity if it were not for Floyd. I never asked him to write that letter. The letter was compelling enough that the Division Commander sent his Assistant Division Commander down to our Unit. The Assistant Division Commander told my Battalion Commander, "Not only will you guys let him go, but you are going to be happy to do it."

So, they released me and I never got hurt by that. I wrestled on the Army Team for two more years. I am forever grateful that I was given that opportunity. Nobody else but Floyd would have gone to bat for me like that.

I was in the Army as an officer, getting paid officer wages, and wrestling for the Service and it was all because of Floyd and that one letter he wrote to the Division Commander. It was life changing for me.

~ Pat Plourd

Dad, I am so proud to call you my father! Over the years you have sacrificed so much for your family. I admire your tenacious work ethic and the eternal sense of security that you provided to your family. There were many nights you rode a bike to work after already working during the day just to put food on the table. You spent many sleepless nights worrying about your children.

Thank you for listening and being that person that I could share my vulnerabilities with over the years. You have always known when to offer me advice or just wipe away my tears.

Floyd Winter, Rick Tucci, and Jennifer Winter (left to right)

Even though you have always shown me your strong and protective side, you have also shown me your softer side and tears. Your unconditional support and encouragement have been monumental in helping me create a fulfilling foundation for my own life.

I respect your integrity and your wisdom. Your strong character has inspired me to value and honor myself. You taught me to be strong and resilient against everything the world throws at my feet. You have been my teacher, not through words, but through actions. You have motivated me to always give everything I do 110%.

You are truly a remarkable man. Looking around today at all the hard work you have put into the CISM games, I could not be prouder. Just like you sacrificed for your family, you also sacrificed for the love of wrestling. People do not often see what goes on behind the scenes to accomplish everything you pulled off. They only get to enjoy all the benefits of your hard work.

I have many childhood memories of watching you coach wrestling. Your passion for the sport was always fascinating to watch!

Your corny jokes, one liners, and never ending supply of t-shirts always bring a smile to my face.

I know that when I brought home a date and you would purposefully call them by a different name, you were not trying to start a fight. You were only trying to weed out the bad apples.

You have always accepted me for who I really was and always saw my true beauty.

Dad, I appreciate you and love you more than you will ever know. After all, I married a man just like you!

No matter what I will always love you and I will always be your girl!

~ Jennifer Winter

I was the Assistant Coach of the All Army Team in 1970 and 1971. I was the Head Coach in 1971 and 1972. I coached two CISM Teams. Floyd was not on the first one, but he was on the second one. That is when he won his gold medal.

I wrestled two years in high school and then I wrestled at the Citadel. I was the Southern Conference Champion. It was not the strongest league; it was a little different from being in the Easterns and things like that.

I was sort of a novice wrestler. I never had a coach at the Citadel. The coach at the Citadel was the low man on the football totem pole. I never had a coach who really wrestled.

Later, I was stationed at Fort Carson, Colorado and I felt like I had not done enough in wrestling. I wrote the Department of Army and said I wanted to try out for the All Army Wrestling Team. I sent my resume that said I was a Conference Champ and that I was the Assistant Coach at the College of William and Mary for two years.

The guy at the Department of Army said, "Well, I see you have coaching experience." He was in charge of different sports not just wrestling. I said, "Well, yeah…" He said, "Would you like to coach?" I was never even in a wrestling clinic! The first wrestling clinic I went to I was coaching at.

He said, "Would you like to coach or wrestle?" I said, "Well, I would like to do both." He replied, "Nope you have to pick one or the other." I opted to coach.

It worked out well. We had a very energetic Head Coach. He was really interested in continuing his competitive career. We had a lot of really good wrestlers because of the draft.

Soldiers were coming from different posts from all over the world to be on the team and wrestle. They had to meet some standards to get to come and then we had to cut the team down. We had Captains, Privates, Majors, Lieutenants, and Sergeants all trying out for the team. It was a real mixture. We had an NCAA Champion and we had Jay Robinson. Jay would eventually help Dan Gable form his whole philosophy at the University of Iowa. It was great for me because we could run our practices like a seminar. Jay was a particularly good technician. We all learned from each other.

When I got out of the Army I wanted to be a coach and I went back to William and Mary as an Assistant. Eventually I became the Head Coach there. I was the Head Coach at East Carolina University. Then I became the Head Coach at the U.S. Military Academy at West Point. I was there all throughout the 1980s.

I have coached a lot of guys who have done good stuff. Out of that crew we had generals, doctors, and lawyers. In 1987 we won the Easterns. When my 167 pounder got out he received a PHD at Princeton, he was an economics guy. He taught at Carnegie Mellon and eventually became George Bush's Economic Adviser. He was the Deputy Secretary of the Treasury. His name is Dr. David McCormick.

I also had a guy named Steve Cannon who got out after serving five years. He was stationed in Berlin and was there when the wall came down. He became fluent in German. He got out of the Army and got a job with Mercedes Benz. I am watching the U.S. Open Tennis Tournament one day and there is this guy giving a check to the winner. It was the CEO of Mercedes Benz North America, Steve Cannon. Steve is now the CEO of AMB Group.

Another wrestler from West Point was Kenny Sullivan. He improved a lot in wrestling with us and became a national qualifier twice. About a year and a half or so ago he sold his energy business for 200 million dollars. We have a legacy from that group at West Point of guys who went on to do great things.

Floyd was unique. We had this one mysterious guy show up at Army Wrestling Camp. He was not a draftee. He was a veteran and had been to Vietnam. He was a little older and from the 82nd Airborne Division. His name was Floyd Winter.

He knew those little nuances that would give his wrestlers the edge. In CISM, in international wrestling there are three referees out there. It can be very political. Our country was centered around college style wrestling, not Freestyle and Greco.

When our wrestlers transitioned they were making a big transition to a different style. Freestyle was different but Greco even more so because there was only upper body wrestling involved. Obviously, Floyd was very good at that. We were fitter than they were. They were bigger than us but we could get them tired and take advantage of that to beat them at the end of the match.

The officials could be very biased. Sometimes wrestlers would stall and we would not get rewarded by them stalling. It could be very frustrating for me as a coach.

Jay Robinson, our Olympian that year, was wrestling a Turk. The Turk was stalling tremendously. Jay was hitting these moves and it would obviously be a two point move for Jay and they would give two points to the other guy. It was very frustrating for us coaching in the corner.

We were in a different environment there. Wayne Baughman and I are getting frustrated because of the way they are officiating Jay. As the match goes on this guy starts stalling really badly and they will not call him stalled. Wayne and I are hollering! All of a sudden these Turkish soldiers came up next to us with machine guns! We said, "Good luck, Jay!" and we sat down.

Although there were no machine guns in Floyd's match, he went through a lot of adversity to be the first American to win Gold in Greco international competition. The Turk he wrestled was obviously stalling too. I am hollering and we are not getting the call or anything like that. To win that medal Floyd had to overcome the officials as well as his opponent who was a Turk, in Turkey, who had a Turkish referee. He managed to overcome a lot of odds to win that gold medal. It was all heart on Floyd's part.

The next day Floyd and I were walking in Ankara, Turkey. We were walking the streets and everyone was pointing at Floyd and saying, "Winter, Winter, Winter!" All the people in the city recognized who he was!

The thing about Floyd is that he has influenced a lot of people. He did it on a grander scale in a lot of ways than myself. He went from a high school wrestler in Porterville, California to someone who was a recognized and respected person in Olympic circles not just nationally, but internationally. What I did was just small potatoes compared to what Floyd has accomplished.

Floyd calls me "Coach" and that is a tremendous honor for me.

~ Ed Steers

Coach has been important in my journey. I met him in Germany while I was in the Army. He came over to do wrestling clinics and watch the athletes who were competing in the European theatre.

He was recruiting athletes he thought were good enough to try out for the All Army Wrestling Team. I did not make the cut the first year. The next year I had improved, especially in Greco which was a new style for me. Floyd was very focused on Greco. I got the chance to go back and try out and I ended up making the team.

This was in 1985. Basically, I spent about six months training with Floyd under his tutelage. We traveled around and competed in various tournaments around the U.S. and internationally. This included the Interservice Championship which obviously is a big deal for bragging rights for the Army against the other services.

I spent the next several years traveling around and wrestling for Coach Winter. I developed the confidence to compete on the international stage and that was largely because of Coach Winter. We had a lot of really good guys and it was a great team. Some of those guys are still my best friends to this day.

A big decision for me was to get out of the Army and take a college scholarship or stay in the Army and keep doing what I was doing with Coach Winter and support my family that way. I was in my mid-twenties and had been in the army for six years. Being an alternate on the Olympic Team got me a lot of attention from the college coaches.

I had to make a decision and could not decide what to do. Coach Winter helped steer me in the right direction. He thought it was better for me not to stay in the Army. That was selfless of him because I had become one of his better athletes at the time. He thought it would be better for me to get out of the service and take that scholarship to get my college education. So, that is what I ended up doing.

Like I said, I never lost touch with a lot of those guys from the All Army Team and with Coach Winter.

That is one of the things I miss most about fighting. I retired from fighting nine years ago, I fought for fourteen years. The fights were something that brought all those guys out. They would come to my MMA fights and that was a chance for us to catch up and see each other.

Randy Couture (left) and Jason Winter

Coach Winter was not a crazy disciplinarian like you might think a wrestling coach would be in the Army. He did have a great system and we never challenged that.

I started a foundation twelve years ago for combat veterans who had been wounded and were in transition. The Army was a very important time for me in my life, wearing that uniform for six years from 19 to 25 years old, and Coach Winter was a big part of that experience.

Now I am at a different stage of my life. Since 9/11 a lot of guys are not just training to fight like I did, but actually having to fight and put their butts on the line. I got to go to Iraq in 2006 and spend time with the soldiers. In 2007 I did a barbeque at the Fisher House at Walter Reed in Washington D.C. I got to walk into the wards and meet a bunch of guys fresh off the battlefield getting physical prosthetics, going through surgeries, trying to get themselves right to transition back to civilian life.

That was a stark experience for me as someone who wore that uniform. I heard their heroic stories and listened to their financial woes. I saw the countless moms, sisters, and wives going there to take care of these guys. So, I started a 501(C)3 called the Extreme Couture GI Foundation.

I raised some money for those guys who were in that situation. It was to take some of the financial pressure off them while they were going through that process and transitioning back to civilian life. We have been doing that for about twelve years.

Every year I go out to the hospital and whatever money we raise goes to the soldiers. Last year we got to help sixteen families. We help anywhere from 10 to 20 families every year. They get a $10,000 check to help them out. It is a way to give back and help some of these guys who have done so much for us.

I first got into wrestling at ten years old when I heard what a great wrestler and tough guy my dad was. So, I thought if I wrestled, he would come around. He never did. He never saw me wrestle a single match. Those coaches filled that void for me. When I needed a kick in the ass they were the guys to do it. They would also throw their arm around me to tell me I did a good job. Coach Winter was one of those guys. He changed me significantly and was, in a lot of ways, a father figure.

~ Randy Couture

I went over to Germany on my first tour in 1977. I got involved in wrestling there by joining a German Club. I started wrestling Greco and Freestyle and that is where I first ran across Floyd. He was stationed in Berlin and was the Head Coach of the Berlin Wrestling Team at the time. It was a very dominant team and he was not only the coach but was wrestling for them as well.

I met Floyd there but I did not know him really well because I wrestled for a different military community. I participated in all those local championships and I wrestled for my German team of course. I ended up going to the U.S. Army Europe Championships a couple of times. I never won them but placed and did okay.

That was it. Then I left Germany in 1980 and went back to the States. I was a Captain at the time stationed at Fort Knox. I decided to apply to the All Army Wrestling Team which was something you did through the DOD Sports Office.

I did not know that Floyd was the Coach of the All Army Team. He invited me to my first trial in 1981 at West Point. I made the team that year and did pretty well for myself. In my mind, when I walked into that team trial and they handed me an All Army Wrestling t-shirt, you could have sent me home and I would have been completely satisfied with my performance. I told myself that I had redeemed myself and my wrestling career. I made the All Army Wrestling Team.

Floyd was such a great coach. He was very knowledgeable and hard charging. He was also approachable, fun, and friendly. At the same time, he worked your ass off. Nobody who was ever on the Army Team with Floyd remembers anything more distinctly than hundreds and hundreds of 200-meter wind sprints on a 400-meter track.

He was a big thrower, that was what he was known for, teaching you to throw. In Greco and Freestyle that is the main thing, being able to throw people. He taught me that. I have to admit, I was not a very good wrestler. I will tell you that straight up. I was an okay wrestler. I placed in the Interservice and I placed in the Nationals one time in Greco. To me that was like, "Oh my God, I can't believe this happened to me!"

In Freestyle I had an arm drag to a single leg. When you first saw me, I could take you down. It did not take you long to figure out this guy has an arm drag to a single leg and you would stop that. That is normally what happened.

In Greco, Floyd taught me throws. He taught me an arm spin, a head and arm, and a couple of good arm throws. I would surprise people. I took some named people and tossed them. I am not saying I beat them, but I tossed them. I felt pretty comfortable with that.

That was what Floyd did for me. He redeemed my wrestling career. To this day if I was to name three or four things in my life that I was extraordinarily proud of, being on the All Army Wrestling Team would be one of those things. I give Floyd all the credit for that.

I had good coaches in high school. I had coaches in college whom I barely remember and they barely remember me. When I got on the All Army Team, Floyd taught me, nurtured me, encouraged me and was extraordinarily good to me. That gave me the confidence and wherewithal to succeed. He let me tell myself, "I'm not a bad wrestler, I can do this!"

I placed in the Interservice, I was second in Greco and third in Freestyle. I went to the National Grecos and placed fourth. I was invited to the World Team. I still have that letter in my scrapbook. I was invited to the World Team Trials! I was not able to go, but I was invited.

Age and injuries caught up with me at 30 years old. Wrestling is a young man's sport. Now, Floyd is a different story. To this day, I would not want to wrestle Floyd. I did not want to wrestle him when I was 26 and I wouldn't want to wrestle him now! He did not look ripped and big, but he was just a phenomenal athlete.

In 1983 a 180-pounder got hurt. He asked my buddy Ted Cuneo, who was the 198-pounder, to go down to 180 pounds, which he did. Floyd had to wrestle at 198 pounds at 36 or 37 years old. I think he won Greco and placed second in Freestyle!

Ted Cuneo (right) (Photo Credit: Cuneo, Ted)

An interesting thing was he was a Non-Commissioned Officer and I was a Captain. The first year I was on the team he knew who I was and I knew who he was. We are not playing this Captain and Sergeant thing. Everybody is on the team and Floyd is the coach.

We were sleeping in the barracks and it was late Saturday night. We are at West Point and we are staying in the Band Barracks. They emptied a big room and we put a bunch of cots and bunk beds for the 25 of us to sleep on. I am sleeping Saturday night and the CQ for the Band comes into the room and says, "Is Captain Diehl in here?" I woke up and said, "What? Yeah, I'm over here."

The kid came over to me and says, "Sir, you need to go to the MP Station and pick up a couple of the wrestlers. They were picked up by the MPs." I said, "I'm one of the wrestlers. I don't have to do that." He replied, "No, Coach Winter called and said to wake you up and tell you to go pick them up." Floyd needed an officer to go do it! So, he recruited me to be the officer to go pick these kids up from the MP Station.

I always thought that was funny! You see, that is why I think he kept me on the team. So that he could have a Captain to send off to do stuff like that.

Floyd just had a phenomenally positive influence on literally hundreds and hundreds of soldiers, officers, and leaders. If you were one of his guys, Floyd Winter would do anything for you.

~ Jim Diehl

I came from a background where my mother was just a dynamo. She was a professional dancer who raised six kids. She had her fifth and sixth children, her second set of twins, at age 40 while going to college. She raised the kids and went back to work full-time as soon as the kids were old enough to be managed. She was also a social butterfly who could read people and was very wise. Floyd was the only person she could never figure out.

1974 was my first year at the All Army Wrestling Camp. I am a Butter Bar Second Lieutenant and Floyd is a Sergeant. One of my other teammates from West Point is also on the team. We are there about three weeks working out two, three or four times a day. Running six miles in the morning, drills, and then wrestle hard in the afternoon. We weightlifted either before dinner or after dinner.

Nobody is leaving post and I am the only one who has a car. I was not supposed to have one. I was almost thrown off the team, before I got on the team, because I brought it and was not supposed to. We liked to play cards at night! Floyd was a gambler and so was I and that is how we took to one another.

He always had a nickname for everybody. We had one guy whose last name was Campbell, so he called him "Soup." I was from West Point which of course is Army so he called me "Big A." Floyd had a name for everybody.

I never had a nickname but I thought, "Whatever." We are playing cards and we are both doing well. However, Floyd has a tendency to win most of the things that he does. Anyway, Floyd said, "We gotta go out!" So, I said, "Okay, let's go out!"

He is a Sergeant and I am a Second Lieutenant. He takes me and my other classmate, another Second Lieutenant, to the Officer's Club to shoot pool. Floyd is a guy so good at pool that you cannot believe it. We go in and have some drinks. He is all about betting and we end up playing some volleyball. Me and my friend are on one side of the net and he is on the other. He beats us two against one.

We sit down and he is ordering drinks. I had smooth screws and my friend was drinking rum and coke. The waitress comes over and Floyd orders five rum and cokes and five smooth screws and whatever he was drinking. Then he says, "And two bottles of champagne, one cold and one warm."

He looks at us and says, "I'm going to give you a chance to win your money back. Double or nothing." By this time, we are kind of psyched out and wondering what he is going to do. He said, "I'm going to pop this cork on one of these bottles of champagne, hit the exit sign at the end of the room with it, then I'm going to drink one bottle of champagne and walk on my hands up to the band." He said he would do all of this in one minute. We are thinking he could probably do it, because he is Floyd Winter, so we said 45 seconds.

He said, "Okay, 45 seconds!" So, he shoots the cork and it did not hit the exit sign but it came close enough so we gave it to him. He downs the bottle of champagne. He then walks up to the band on his hands going in-between tables. He did this all in under 45 seconds. He did it and knew he could do it closer to 30 seconds! I never bet against the guy after that.

I never, ever had a bad time with Floyd. He was such a caring person. His number one thing was to make you feel comfortable and get you to laugh. He loved to entertain. I never heard him brag, he was not a showboat. It was always just fun stuff.

In high school I was a good student and athlete but I did not excel at anything. I tried track, baseball, basketball, and football. I was okay at them but they did not have wrestling at my high school until I was a sophomore. I took to it right away. Unfortunately, I broke my wrist the first year but the next two years I did well.

I qualified for the State Tournament. I did not do well but it was interesting. The principal was a former wrestler and we hit it off. He made an announcement that I was the only one to qualify for that tournament. They hardly ever made announcements like that.

I was good all around, I was the Captain of the Wrestling Team, Sergeant of Arms in the Key Club, and President of the Marching Band. That is what West Point wants. Somebody who is good all-around and who is a leader. So, I applied to West Point. They had Division 1 wrestling and I got in.

I was not the best cadet. I was very disciplined but when you have it imposed upon you it is different. I understood though, it was the military after all. I graduated and I was at my basic course, field artillery and I ran into a guy who was on the West Point Wrestling Team. He was a year ahead of me. I said, "What are you doing?" He said, "I'm in the infantry but right now I'm on the All Army Wrestling Team." So, I said, "Oh wow, how do you get on that?" He told me I had to write a letter and request it.

I wrote a letter to my unit to be, which I had never been to, and said that I wanted to be on the wrestling team. I got there and I am a second Lieutenant and the Colonel calls me into his office. He said, "Listen Lieutenant, you ain't going into any goddamn weightlifting team!" I said, "Sir, it's a wrestling team." He replied, "I don't care what the

F**k it is, you work for me, you got it!?" I responded, "Yes, Sir!"

We had a new General who wore pearl-handled 45s like a cowboy. He loved sports. He introduced combat football, which was 100 or more people on the field tackling one another. He also introduced combat basketball, I never happened to see a game because I was not a big fan.

Everybody was supposed to get up and run every morning. The first week that he was there, they had three heart attacks. You had cooks who had not run a mile since who knows when. Anyway, so I sent my request through my Colonel up to the General. The General said, "Hell yeah, he's goin'!"

I went into the Colonel's Office and he said, "Lieutenant, I don't care if I ever see you again. Here are your orders. Get out of here!" I thought, "Yes!"

I was supposed to take a flight but I wanted to bring my car. I had a Corvette. West Point cadets were not allowed to have a car until their senior year. I brought my car and I got caught. They were going to kick me off the team that I was not even on yet.

Luckily, the coach was entertaining the Sports Director from Washington D.C. The coach did not have access to a car. He ended up asking me to use my car and because of that I was allowed to stay. I got so lucky! My life would have turned out so much different if I had been kicked out.

Other than my 30 years with my wife, those were the best four years of my life. A large part of that was because of Floyd. He was the only guy whom I have ever met who really kept in touch with his buddies from the past. He would call me regularly and always keep in touch. I said to myself, "I really like this guy."

He called me up in-between the season when I was back in my Unit. He called up and said, "This is Sergeant Winter and I'd like to speak to Lieutenant Grunseth." They said, "Sergeant Winter, he's not available" before they even looked for me.

The next time Floyd called he said, "This is Captain Winter. Can I speak to Lieutenant Grunseth?" They replied, "We will look for him, Sir."

Floyd called again and said, "This is Colonel Winter. I want to speak to Lieutenant Grunseth." This time they replied, "Yes, Sir! Yes, Sir! Right away! He will be here in 10 seconds!"

Who would do that!? They hand me the phone and say, "It is Colonel Winter." I replied, "Okay, I know him, thank you" so they would walk away. I was laughing my ass off. Floyd said, "You know, you gotta adapt." Floyd is just a clever guy and quick with the retort.

I was double dating with my girlfriend and Floyd and Paula. We go out to dinner and there is still snow and ice on the ground. In the parking lot, Floyd slips and falls.

My girlfriend, instead of saying "Are you all right?" says "Your hair is askew." He is not even up from the ground yet and Floyd says, "Well, *askew* me!" It was a play on words but I do not know how he thought of that so quickly! He had perfect timing and said it with a straight face.

We are at the camp when he met Paula and all of a sudden he is not coming to morning practice. Which was unheard of. With the coach we had for two of the years he would not have gotten away with it, but we had a weak coach and he let him get away with it for some reason.

Later in 1975, Paula and Floyd were going to get married so we went out to San Francisco. We were at a restaurant where his high school buddy and best friend used to work. We are in this restaurant and his best friend Web is there. Web is straightforward and looks at Floyd and says, "You know Floyd, I don't think you should get married right now."

Paula is sitting there and her face is burning. We all get in the car to leave. Paula is in the back with her girlfriend and Floyd and I are in the front. I am driving.

I am going across the Bay Bridge doing maybe 45 MPH. Floyd locks his door with his elbow as he rolls down his window. He then crawls out onto the hood of the car while we are going 45 MPH over the Bay Bridge! He is standing up and starts dancing on the hood of the car! I am freaking out. I do not want to brake so I just take my foot off the gas to gradually slow down.

We were surrounded by cars on all sides and they all just moved away like in a cartoon or something. Floyd crawls back in and Paula says, "Do I want to marry this guy?" I said, "Floyd, what the hell are you doing?" He said, "I didn't see any sign that said no dancing!"

Floyd wrestles with no socks, which kind of looks funny. He goes to weigh in and he does not wear a jock strap. He strips down and he is naked. We are all just looking at him. I never understood that because he never had trouble making weight!

Here is a guy who weighed about 195 pounds. When he worked out hard during the season he was maybe 193 pounds. He never cut weight. He was so good that he would wrestle 198 pounds against guys who were monsters cutting down from 210 to 215 pounds. He would even wrestle 220 pounds. He had such a good headlock that he would catch these guys.

A guy was trying out for the team. He is a heavyweight and he has to wrestle off some of the returning All Army Wrestlers. Floyd is wrestling this big guy who weighs at least 230 pounds. This guy's training meal was a six pack of beer and an extra-large pizza. He was a happy go lucky guy though, a fun guy.

A lot of people who are right-handed throw their headlock by grabbing with the left and throw with the right. Floyd could do it on both sides but he did it more on the left side with the underhook. That threw people off.

They are on the mat wrestling and Floyd hits his first headlock. Floyd lets him go to stand back up. The guy jumps up and says, "You are not going to catch me again!" I signaled to Floyd to throw the headlock on the other side. Ten seconds later he catches the guy in a headlock on the other side. This happened about six times. The guy would jump up and say, "You aren't going to do that to me again!" Floyd would just switch up and do right, left, left, left, right and he would catch him every time.

In those four years I was on the All Army Wrestling Team I did so many fun things that were memorable for me. Many of those things were done with Floyd Winter. He was so consistent in helping family and friends. He could not do enough for you. I told him, "Floyd, you have to accept something back from people." He responded, "I just like to help." There was no quid pro quo with him. He is just a giving guy. It was just pure goodness of heart.

~ Marc Grunseth

I am African American. My father passed away in 1964 when I was five years old. I remember my father used to roll around and wrestle with me. He had wrestled in college. When he passed away at 32 years old, I think he was like 30 hours away from getting his doctorate. Back in those days that was really rare.

I went blank for a while after he died. When I was in elementary school there was a special program for wrestling. So, I got into wrestling. I remember my mother telling me, "You know, your dad wrestled."

It just continued from elementary school to middle school. My last year of middle school, my friend and I were good enough to make the high school team. After school we would go to the high school for practice. Long story short, I was the first one in the history of my high school to make it to the State Championships. Unfortunately, I came in 3rd place.

I wanted to continue to wrestle in college. I had a full scholarship to wrestle at Morgan State University in Baltimore, Maryland. It is a Historical Black University. Our team was awesome! I was a two-time NCAA All American.

During college I went to an ROTC program and I got commissioned as an officer. I graduated and I ended up going to Germany. I was excited because I wanted to continue to wrestle and I knew in Europe, especially in Germany, they were pretty good wrestlers in Greco-Roman.

I wrestled in my off time. They had what is called the USAREUR Championships. I wrestled both styles, Freestyle and Greco. Coach Winter was there scouting for the All Army Wrestling Team. He came from the United States to recruit American wrestlers in Germany.

I won Freestyle and Greco. He asked me, "Do you want to come back to the States and try out for the All Army Team?" I responded, "Yes, I do!" He gave me the opportunity to fulfill my dream, which was to make the Olympic Team and win a gold medal.

I absolutely jumped on that opportunity. It was a little unique because I was an officer and I had to get permission from my commanders to allow me to leave. I was a Platoon Leader at the time.

I went over and I made the All Army Team. I met up with my other teammates at Fort Campbell. They were Randy Couture, Derrick Waldroup, Gary Barber, and a bunch of other guys. Gary Barber was a huge guy and he was a helicopter pilot! I was like, "How the hell do you fit in a helicopter!?"

That whole experience of being out there at Fort Campbell was really unique. For six weeks of training Coach Winter had people from all over the United States and different bases internationally coming in. Thank God, I made the team.

I will never forget there was a guy from California. We wrestled off each other maybe five or six times. I ended up losing and this was at around 182.5 pounds. I knew I was going to be cutting weight because I wrestled at 119 pounds in high school and 150 pounds in college.

Floyd knew that I was going to cut weight and go down to 163 pounds. Floyd said, "Why don't you challenge at 220 pounds?" I was not going to beat Randy Couture or Derrick Waldroup. I challenged at 220 pounds and I made the team.

We went to the Armed Forces Championships in Sacramento, California. The first match I had to wrestle was a Marine. I will never forget it! I weighed 180 pounds and this guy weighed 220 pounds and I think he was a silver medalist in the Olympics. He was a legend for the Marines, his name was Greg Gibson.

The first match was Greco-Roman. The whistle blew and he came at me and I arm spun him and threw him to his back. The crowd went, "Ewww!" I could not hold him down because he was so much bigger than I was. I ended up losing the match but I came back and got a Bronze Medal.

The same thing happened the next tournament that was a day later. I had him the first match in Freestyle. I could see this weird look in his eyes. Coach Winter put me up to this but if it weren't for him, I wouldn't be there. Greg Gibson came at me and I threw him to his back. The crowd went, "Ewww!" again. I ended up losing again though because I could not hold him down.

Coach Winter and I really clicked. When we had a little bit of a break, I would go out to have a beer with him. We both loved playing pool so we would team up and play pool. We would be getting tore up because we would always win and be playing for drinks! We did not have to pay for anything! He would be tore up and could still walk on his hands on the pool table and up and down stairs. It was amazing the things he could do.

Coach was something else. He has lived several full lives. I have been blessed in the world of wrestling. I fell short of being an Olympic alternate for Barcelona, but I would not trade it for the world for the experiences I have had. Floyd is like a father figure to me.

I was there to wrestle. I did my damnedest to put the work in to accomplish my dream and take advantage of the opportunity that Floyd gave me. I tried to make the most of it. Us wrestlers were close. All of us were like siblings. We would argue and fight or whatever, but the love was there.

With me being a married officer, I got housing on post. Once I got housing on post I would invite the whole team over. Most of them were staying in the barracks and a lot of them were single.

My wife is German and she loves to cook. I would have them over to eat. The soldiers felt like they were at home. I used to do that so they would have some home cooked meals instead of the mess hall all of the time. It was also team bonding. After practice, or if we had a couple of days off when Coach gave us a break, we would go swim laps in the pool or go fishing and just kind of hang out.

Floyd is so unique and I love the guy. Every now and then he reaches out to me or I reach out to him. I am sure other guys have a special bond with him but I know our friendship is special. I truly appreciate him for all that he has done for me.

~ Phil Brown

I was born and raised in western Pennsylvania. In the 1960s it was a pretty big hotbed for wrestling. I got involved in wrestling at the age of about five or six.

I moved through high school and wrestled in college. I left college and joined the Army and went to Europe. I was looking for something to do. I could not do football anymore, but Jimmy Diehl was on the same post and we linked up and started wrestling.

Jimmy and I would go around Europe and wrestle in these tournaments. We had some decent success except for when we ran into the Berlin Brigade guys.

The Berlin Brigade guys were coached by none other than Floyd "Bad News" Winter. They were loaded. Floyd was in my weight class. While I was in Europe, I think I lost six times. Five of them were to Floyd. He used a different technique each time.

I had wrestled 200 to 300 matches in my career so far when I wrestled Floyd for the second time. He pinned me and I was not used to getting pinned. He had two devastating moves. One was a headlock and the other one was a three-quarter Nelson. When he got it and cranked it with leverage, either you went over or he was going to break something.

We were wrestling in Berlin and for some reason I still think I have a chance against Floyd. When I grabbed onto him it was like grabbing a steel cable. For the first 30 or 40 seconds we were pushing back and forth. He sets me up and hits me with a headlock. I knew it was going to end badly, but I was so impressed because it was one of the best headlocks I had ever seen or been involved with.

It just so happened that I was on the receiving end of this one. When I hit I immediately knew I did something wrong. Jimmy Diehl was in my corner for that match. As soon as I came off the mat after Floyd pinned me, I said, "Hey Jim, I think I broke my shoulder."

I went and got some x-rays. I had broken and separated it. My collarbone was broke and I separated my shoulder at the same time. While the result was painful, as I was going through the air, I was so impressed that it was like the perfect headlock. It was one of those love/hate things, I guess.

At that time, I did not know Floyd very well. The big thing for those U.S. Army tournaments for me and Jim were that if you ranked pretty high or you won the USAREUR, you stood a pretty good chance of getting invited back to the All Army Camp. Floyd would bring like forty guys back and you would train for six to eight weeks. Then Floyd would select the top 20 wrestlers.

You would continue to wrestle and if you did well in the Interservice Tournaments then you would progress. You would go to some National Tournaments. Then, maybe, by chance you might get an invite to the Olympic Trials or something like that. Some guys were very good and able to do that and some guys reached their talent level and moved on.

Floyd ran the hell out of us and his whistle never stopped blowing. I am built for comfort not speed. I hated to run. I hated every step. However, when I left the camp I ran the fastest mile and two mile I ever ran in my life. I ran a six-minute mile and when I came back and took the Army PT I ran an 11 or 12 two mile. I never got close to that again, before or after. That was the best shape that I was ever in my life. That was thanks to Floyd. He would draw the absolute best out of you. I do not know how to describe it, but he did it in a way that just made you want to do it.

Until I went to Europe I always wrestled collegiate. I had never wrestled Greco or Freestyle. Sambo came into the picture in the 1980s. I think that was kind of the forerunner to UFC ultimately. The Russians developed Sambo. It was a combination between Judo and you had submission holds and all that sort of stuff. Floyd could do all that.

He beat World Class wrestlers. He beat Greg Gibson the year before I was on the Army Team. Either then, or soon after that, Gibson was rated the #1 wrestler in the world. Floyd hit him with one of his patented headlocks. He was just an amazing athlete. He is probably the most amazing athlete I have ever come across.

Greg Gibson (right), USMC, 1982

His athletic talent was one thing, but honestly he was just a great guy to be around! He was funny as hell. I was playing him in racquetball one time. I was not the greatest racquetball player but I had played for about six to eight years and I was okay. I am playing him and I have him 19–3.

He stopped and gave me one of those looks and says, "I'll bet you…" I do not remember exactly what we bet but I remember thinking, "There is no way he is going to beat me. I can get two more points on this guy." Long story short, Floyd beat me. I have thought about that a lot, if Floyd was just playing with me the whole time. However, I do not think so. I don't think he was sandbagging me. With Floyd if he bet you something, that competitive spirit would come out, and it was just an amazing thing.

Ted Cuneo, Gary Barber, and Jim Diehl (left to right)

He was also inspirational. He was one of those guys you had as a coach who you wanted to do your absolute best for. He would not do it by badgering you or anything else. You just respected and liked him and did not want to disappoint him. He was never disappointed though; he was always uplifting. He would try to help you with what went wrong or what went right.

He guided us to success that we otherwise would not have had.

He is an amazing athlete, an amazing human being, and a dear friend.

~ Ted Cuneo

The first time I met Floyd was in the finals of the New York Athletic Club Christmas Tournament. We were both headlockers. He had a headlock and I had a headlock. He is left handed and I am right handed. We are essentially like two mirror images of each other.

I was wrestling for the NY Athletic Club and he was wrestling for the Army. I headlocked him and I ended up hurting him. Not deliberately, we were both just physical guys, and one of us happened to get hurt.

I never thought much of it but he always remembered that. I ended up winning the match. Floyd then heard that I was in the Army. He called me up while I was in my medical internship down in Georgia and I am working about 110 hours a week.

Floyd told me, "I want you to wrestle for the U.S. Army." I told him, "Floyd, I don't even see my family, there is no way I can wrestle for the Army!" I told him I would not be able to wrestle for him until I am out of my residency. Floyd said, "Okay, I will remember that."

I get stationed at West Point. Sure enough, I get a phone call from old Floyd to wrestle on the All Army Team.

I peaked in wrestling while I was in medical school. I got accepted to medical school but had a year off. I was pre-med at Cornell and the Captain of the wrestling team. I worked out three hours a day and had to study my ass off and go to all my classes. I finished in four years, I did not delay anything or take summer courses. I just went through it and did it.

I was Captain of my team sophomore, junior, and senior year. I got accepted to medical school but since I had a year off, I was like, "Well, I am going to wrestle five hours a day." I got really good that way. I was ranked top three in the U.S. and made the U.S. Olympic Team. I got really good based on that one year where I could focus on training.

So, I stuck with it in medical school and I talked to Floyd here and there. In 1978 while I was in medical school I won a National Freestyle tournament. Floyd got a hold of me in 1979 after I graduated. He said, "Hey, you told me to get back in touch with you!"

I told Floyd I still had to get through my internship and residency. I did that and he got back in touch with me again. He said, "Okay, you are out of your residency now, you can start wrestling for the All Army Team."

The first year I wrestled for the Army was 1983 and he was my coach. The Army Team would work out for six weeks. The Marines always finished first because they trained all year around. The Army usually came in second.

I was working out with the cadets at West Point and told Floyd, "Listen, I am a doctor up here, I can't go to a six-week camp." Floyd said, "Listen, you come for the last week of the camp. I will have a wrestle off during that last week and if you win that you are on the team. You will only have to beat one guy. If you lose to your guy you go back home to West Point."

I said, "That is not very fair. The guys have been at the camp for six weeks and I walk in the last week. I don't think the other guys on the team are going to like me very much. I am coming in the last week like some kind of prima donna." Floyd said, "I think that they will understand that you are a doctor. I think they will understand the situation." I said, "Well, I will still feel bad for the guy if I beat him in the wrestle off." Floyd replied, "Well, don't feel too bad otherwise you aren't going to beat him!" So, I said, "Okay, Floyd."

I go to the camp and I am in pretty good shape because I was working out with the cadets. I ended up beating the guy in the wrestle off and I made the team. I am working out a lot with the guy who is ranked number one. I was like 31 or 32 years old. Floyd was six years older than me. I am working out with Floyd and this number one guy and I told Floyd this guy is pretty good. Floyd said, "Yeah, he's okay." Floyd thought I still had some good matches left in me, despite my age.

We are at the tournament and it is in Quantico. There was a Marine who won it two or three times already in my weight class. I heard about him, that he was a good wrestler. Floyd came back with a big smile on his face and said, "I got you seated right where I want you." I thought good, he probably got me first or second seat. I said, "Where did you get me seated?" He said, "You got the eighth seat out of eight people."

I said, "What!?" Floyd responded, "Yeah, they didn't know who you were. They knew nothing about you. This is perfect!" I looked at him like he was nuts. He continued, "You're wrestling the number one seed right off the bat. And you know what? You are going to beat him! But guess what? This guy has been training every day for a year and is a beast. He has three coaches and I'm just here by myself. They would have figured you out if you wrestled him in the finals. You are going to wrestle him in the first round and he's not going to know what hit him!" I said, "Okay, Floyd, I will trust your judgment."

I wrestled him the first round and I beat him 8–3. At that point I realized Floyd was a genius. How many coaches would have had enough sense to know that? Not only did he set it up, but he convinced me that it would work and it did.

I am still very close to wrestling and help out at Blair Academy, which is the number one team in the country. I have a daughter who is a two-time Canadian National Champion in wrestling. She is home now because of this COVID thing and she has me working out with her twice a day.

~ Dr. Walter Grote

Floyd has impacted my life in many ways. For example, I am now a college wrestling coach. I wrestled at Indiana State. When I got done wrestling, I said there are two things I never want to do again; wrestle or do manual labor. People told me I should be a high school coach. But I never wanted to coach wrestling.

I think Floyd had lots of recruiters and feelers out there. I was sitting in a bar in Indiana just drinking a beer by myself. In comes an Army recruiter. He sits next to me and asks me how I am doing. We were drinking a little bit and he asked me if I ever thought about the military.

I said my dad was in the Navy and I thought about it but I don't think it is for me. We kept drinking and the next thing he said was, "You know, you could wrestle in the Army." I said, "You know what? If you can get me a try out for the All Army Wrestling Team I'll go check it out."

A week later this recruiter guy pulls up to my house. He said, "Hey, I have that set up for you tomorrow. Are you good?" The next day I drive down to the All Army Wrestling Camp. I walk in and I have hair down to the middle of my back. Everybody was looking at me like, "Who is this guy?"

Floyd asked me, "What do you weigh?" I said, "About 172 or 175 pounds but I wrestle at 136.5 pounds." Floyd looked at me and said, "When you get down there, we will let you wrestle at 136.5 pounds!" The first guy I wrestled was Tony Thomas. Tony is a lot bigger than me. He hits an arm spin on me and throws me halfway across the mat.

The next guy was a 149-pounder. I think it was Bobby Good. Bobby goes to lock up on me and I throw him on his back. Floyd said, "I've seen enough. You can try out for our team." I went home and the recruiter was like, "Are you ready to sign? Are you ready to sign?"

Sure enough they got me signed up. I made the All Army Team and wrestled for two years. I placed at the Interservice Tournaments. Floyd had a real impact on me because when I got out of the Army I went to Missouri and became the Head Wrestling Coach at Truman State University. I have been there for 29 years and have always had a picture of Floyd up on our wall in our wrestling room.

One time my Captain told me, "You need to make sure you come back after leave." I replied, "No, the All Army Coach told me I am going to go to Colorado Springs." My Captain became irate. He told me I was AWOL and they were sending the MPs to come get me. I was AWOL for about sixty days. Floyd told me, "Don't worry about it. I'll take care of it." Floyd picked up the telephone and called somebody and it was all cleared up.

I hurt my neck and ended up having to get C-4, C-5 surgery. That was right during All Army Camp. They sent me to Fort Campbell's hospital and they said they did not find anything and sent me back to practice. Floyd sent me back to the hospital and told them something was wrong with me.

Then they sent me to Vanderbilt and they did an MRI and found I had a crushed vertebrae. If Floyd had not pushed to get me looked at further, I could have gotten really hurt.

Floyd always took care of us really well and how he took care of us is how I take care of my athletes at Truman.

~ David Schutter

I met Neil in the fifth grade and we have been best friends ever since. I call him by his middle name "Neil", while most people know him as Floyd. He has always had my back and I have always had his. We were both just really good at friendship. I know him better than anybody except for maybe his wife.

We were playing pool one time with some of our buddies above Porterville, where we grew up. It was a bar called "The Antlers." It was a very well-known country bar that had been there a long time. One night Neil said to the bartender, "I'll bet you I can chug two beers, walk around these two pool tables on my hands, and then back in one minute." I do not know what he bet him.

I did not think he could do it, to be honest with you. But I knew him well enough not to bet against him. Neil did it in 45 seconds. Everybody was like, "Oh my God!" First of all, people do not usually walk on their hands, especially after chugging two beers. The story is still a legend in that bar.

The more he drinks, the better he gets at playing pool. He would be beating guys and they were going to quit. Then he would say, "Well, I'll use a broom or a mop." Of course, they would take that bet and he would do just about as good with a broom or a mop. He was always better when there was something on the line like money.

When we would go to sporting events in high school, on the bus we would play cards. There was a game called Pitch which I do not even remember how to play. Anyway, we had a system designed on how to cheat. One person who had a terrible hand would bid a certain amount. You would have had to have a good hand to bid that. He knew what I had and I knew what he had. People would watch us and make sure our feet were not touching, trying to figure out how we did it. Nobody was ever able to figure out what we were doing. It was a pretty clever system we had.

Neil is a very unique person there is no question about that. He carved out his own unique career in the Army. He kind of invented his own position you might say.

We were both out of the Army and he came to stay with me in San Francisco. It was a little place down by the Civic Center. I had a gun in the closet and someone broke in and stole it, among other things.

I was a bartender and Neil was working as a security guard at the time. The gun was used in a crime and since it was registered they contacted me. I ended up having to go to a trial in San Jose and Neil went with me. The lawyer had me up on the stand and wanted to know how I could prove it was mine. I said, "Well it is registered in my name." They asked why I had it and I said, "For protection, but now I have a security guard living with me." Everyone laughed.

His wife Paula likes to call herself my little sister. She is like a sister to me. I can talk to her about anything. I have lived with both of them on numerous occasions. Paula is a fabulous cook and makes these huge elaborate meals. She uses every single pot and pan in the building. So, I always feel like the least I can do is the dishes. The running joke is that she purposefully uses every pot and pan and takes inventory so I can wash them. So, when I talk to her I always say, "I sure miss your cooking but not your pots and pans!" She is actually the best cook I have ever known.

Neil is a very good chess player. We learned how to play it together. He used to go this park and play chess with all the people there. One time this mutual friend of ours, who was kind of a brainiac, came over and was talking about how good of a chess player he was. We were all in high school at the time.

Neil said, "Really? I've always wanted to learn how to play chess." Our friend said, "Well, I'll show you!" He got his chess set out and was explaining this is how the pawn moves etc. Neil said to him, "I think I got it. Let's try a game out." Long story short, Neil beat him. Our friend realized he had gotten taken and knocked the chess set across the room.

Another time Neal was on an airplane. There was a master or grandmaster chess player, whatever you call them, on the airplane. The guy made an announcement if anyone on the plane knew how to play chess and several people raised their hands. He had seven or eight different games going all at the same time on the airplane.

He would just go from one board to the other making his moves instantaneously. He beat everyone else on the plane he was playing but Neil. He was the last one standing. He ended up beating Neil too but it was pretty amazing.

Neil and I would joke around about what an ideal woman or guy was. For an ideal guy we would say Steve McQueen or Paul Newman. For an ideal woman it would be Raquel Welch or Natalie Wood. We would be at a bar and I would say, "Hey, do you think she is as good looking as Natalie Wood?" That type of thing.

Neil and I were living in San Francisco in the Tenderloin. We would go down to Market Street and pay a dollar to see a couple of movies. Then we would pay another dollar for an all you can eat Chinese buffet. That is what we did a lot of the time during the day.

I had a post office box in the post office down by Market St. & 7th. It was across the street from the Greyhound Bus

Depot where all these different winos and derelicts hung out. We were walking to go get my mail one day and I see these two winos across the street fighting each other.

Just to be funny I said to Neil, "Hey, do those two guys remind you of Steve McQueen?" I was just trying to be ridiculous. Neil looked over there and said, "Hey, that is Steve McQueen!" I looked over there again and standing about ten feet away from the winos fighting was in fact Steve McQueen. What were the chances of that! We walked over there and told him he was our favorite actor and he shook our hands.

While we lived in San Francisco I had a little Volkswagen bug. We were driving across the Oakland Bay Bridge and Brown Eyed Girl was playing on the radio. Neil crawls out the passenger-side window onto the hood of the Volkswagen while I am driving 60 MPH over the bridge at night. He stood up and was dancing the boogaloo! I did not slow down because I was scared any change could make him fall. I just held the wheel steady. One slight little mishap and he would have been dead.

That was the kind of stuff he used to do. He was very daring and was a risk taker.

About ten years ago, Neil and I had lunch with a girl we went to high school with. She is a retired lawyer and her husband is a retired judge. She mentioned that she had the idea of starting a Vietnam War Memorial Scholarship for our high school to honor the three guys in our high school who were killed in Vietnam. Neil and I agreed that would be a good thing.

It was her idea and the three of us started it. I would write the blurb that we would send out to all the classmates so that they could donate money. We have gotten money every year, like $3,000 to $4,000. Neil would fly out and do the presentation since he is a Vietnam Veteran. We have done it every year for ten years.

For the last several years, Neil and I have talked almost every day on the phone. It has pretty much been every single day with the rare exception.

Neil has had a huge impact on my life. In over sixty years of knowing each other we have never had an argument or disagreement.

We are closer than most brothers.

The bottom line is that we have always been the best of friends. He has taken care of me and I have tried to take care of him.

~ Webbie Loyd

About the Author

Daniel DiMarzio was born on the Army Base in Fort Campbell, Kentucky, in 1982. He graduated from Peirce College in 2006 with a Bachelor of Science in Business Administration, Concentration in Management, and is a member of Delta Mu Delta, International Honor Society in Business Administration. He is also a graduate of the Pennsylvania School of Muscle Therapy.

Daniel is the author of numerous books investigating cultures around the world.

His books are available in stores worldwide. They can also be found in public libraries from Dubai to Kathmandu and beyond.